T0065207

BERTHA'S WORD

THE STORY OF THE JEWISH FORTUNE TELLER WHO BROUGHT DOWN NAZI GERMANY

BASED ON A TRUE STORY

DANNY RITTMAN

BERTHA'S WORD
THE STORY OF THE JEWISH FORTUNE TELLER
WHO BROUGHT DOWN NAZI GERMANY

Copyright © 2021 Danny Rittman.

All rights reserved. No part of this book may be used or reproduced by any means,
graphic, electronic, or mechanical, including photocopying, recording, taping or by
any information storage retrieval system without the written permission of the author
except in the case of brief quotations embodied in critical articles and reviews.

iUniverse books may be ordered through booksellers or by contacting:

iUniverse
1663 Liberty Drive
Bloomington, IN 47403
www.iuniverse.com
844-349-9409

Because of the dynamic nature of the Internet, any web addresses or links contained in
this book may have changed since publication and may no longer be valid. The views
expressed in this work are solely those of the author and do not necessarily reflect the
views of the publisher, and the publisher hereby disclaims any responsibility for them.

Any people depicted in stock imagery provided by Getty Images are models,
and such images are being used for illustrative purposes only.
Certain stock imagery © Getty Images.

ISBN: 978-1-6632-2789-8 (sc)
ISBN: 978-1-6632-2790-4 (e)

Library of Congress Control Number: 2021917206

Print information available on the last page.

iUniverse rev. date: 09/07/2021

"וּבָא עָלַיִךְ רָעָה לֹא תֵדְעִי שַׁחְרָהּ וְתִפֹּל עָלַיִךְ הֹוָה לֹא תוּכְלִי כַּפְּרָהּ
וְתָבֹא עָלַיִךְ פִּתְאֹם שׁוֹאָה לֹא תֵדָעִי."

ישעיהו מ"ז:י"א

"Yet shall evil came upon thee; Thou shalt not know how to charm it away;
And calamity shall fall upon thee; Thou shalt not be able to put it away;
And ruin shall come upon thee suddenly, Before thou knowest."

Isaiah 47:11

"Just because you have never seen a miracle, it doesn't mean it doesn't exist."

MY DREAM

J ust in front of me stood a tyrant – a man the entire world feared. He symbolized madness, war, and death. His eyes were a dark tunnel to his soul. He stood there and waited for my response. He waited to hear what the future held for him and his plans. However, I was mesmerized and feared any words I might speak or thoughts I might have would give him more power and will – fuel for his immense and spreading fire.

"I will triumph. I will become master. Everyone will know my name for all time. I am eternal."

I struggled to get hold of myself and find the words to fight back against his return. I gathered my being and began to shout a response:

"You are not alive! You died long ago and will never return!"

"I am eternal. I am always with you, never far away. Look around, look inside."

Black legions gathered behind him from all corners of the world and changed from mobs to orderly ranks and file.

"Look around, look inside. Look around, look inside. Look around, look inside."

I woke up in a start. My wife told me this happened several times over the last few weeks, then went back to sleep.

I needed to talk to someone.

MY FRIEND

I made an appointment to visit Bertha. She always welcomed me with a broad, genuine smile from one high cheekbone to the other and bid me enter her home.

Such an elegant woman! Her gray hair and mysterious green eyes told of long years, many of them hard and even tragic. Yet, her demeanor was always cheerful least near me. Ever in colorful dresses and silver broaches and earrings and when she walked across a room in her house she did so barefoot and her gait was so light as to suggest hovering rather than walking.

Most people her age in Israel had adopted modern surroundings fashioned in the new country after World War Two but Bertha was clearly Old Europe. Her dwelling not far from the coast was furnished with exotic items such as old clocks and detailed mahogany furniture and Indian cloths and rugs from the Middle East.

Her peers had accents from Hungary and the Ukraine but hers was clearly German, south German to be specific. It was easy to envision her an urbane, well-educated young woman at an opera or gallery. Easy for me at least. Most of her neighbors did not know what to make of her and knew only that she was a mystic of some sort.

"Dani!" she exclaimed. "Please be seated wherever you will. Ah, but you like the settee, of course. I'll have your cappuccino anon." She'd sit down across from me ask me to show her my hands. "Young man, what's on your mind today?" With that, she gently nodded towards the elegant porcelain jar and I place few bills into it, smiling to myself. Business as usual.

She'd become quiet and look carefully at my hands, studying every line and prominence until perceptions and thoughts came across her mind like sun and shadow on a meadow in late afternoon. My eyes must have conveyed much, as they do to anyone. Bertha's perceptions were far more keen. She read my state of mind, my hopes, disappointments, and worries. Her hands rested on my temples as we spoke, urging me on and healing me. How could she know so much about me?

"Your dream is not unusual. Many people here have similar ones though they are usually closer to my age than yours. It is a good sign. You are aware of the world and its perils. One day I will tell you of an experience I had long ago back in Germany just after the war."

"I look forward to that."

"Not too soon, Dani. Not too soon."

My heart found joy in its inner recesses. All this in an hour's time. She concluded readings with calming thoughts always ending with "Bertha's word".

Someone in hi-tech isn't supposed to put stock in fortune telling. Few colleagues appreciate the artistry and spirituality at the outer fringes of science. Chip design challenges me and pays the bills but I wander outside walls whenever I can. Over the decades Bertha had so many more important clients than the computer engineer before her that day and her readings left a trace on those dreadful years in Europe, though of course not as much as she wanted.

The readings became conversations and chats and in time, revelations. I was more than a client. Bertha loved me. I could read that easily enough. If she hadn't loved me, she wouldn't have read me so well. Nor would she have trusted me with her story with all its courage and tragedy.

When I stopped by unannounced a month later something was amiss. A woman of some age though much younger than Bertha opened the door. Her sadness was clear and it concerned me.

"Oh, excuse me. Is Bertha here? I am a regular and —"

"I am so sorry. sir, but she is in the hospital."

Her voice was soft and solemn and the words came with difficulty.

"The hospital! I saw her only.... I'm so sorry."

"Two days ago it was. She collapsed two days ago. At home. The doctors aren't optimistic and she knows her time is at hand."

My heart sank.

"I want to see her."

"Young man, don't you understand?"

"It's not that. Bertha is a friend and I need to see her, even if the hour is late for her. Please tell her that Daniel needs to see her. She'll know the name, though she calls me 'Dani'."

She weighed my words and studied my face. "I am her daughter. I'll speak with her this evening and convey your wishes. But the hour is late, as you said. Leave your number."

The door closed.

"Never knew Bertha had family."

The daughter called me the next day and without even telling me her name, gave me the welcome word.

When I arrived at the hospital her daughter was waiting just inside the entrance. She led me into Bertha's room and there she was, elegant as always despite the ordeal of the last few days and the grim prospects. Neat and graceful, cheeks rosy with vigor and joy and all the brighter in the white room. She brightened on seeing me and that gladdened me.

"Dani, so good to see you, my young friend. Thank you so much for coming. How are you doing, dear?"

"Bertha, what happened?"

"What happened is what happens to us all. The particulars of my case are not at all important. The important matter is what lies ahead. Ordinarily, I say little or nothing. That's my way. But I see

4

the doctors' faces and listen to their reports and though they don't say it, I know what's coming in the next few days. I usually do. Now, Dani, you know as well."

I stood in sorrow and helplessness. She was my psychic, yes. She was also a friend, a guide, practically a parent. I respected her and loved her and I had no words to convey my sorrow. That was clear to all in the room.

"Dani, I agreed to see you today because I consider you very special." She looked into my heart and continued. "I have an unusual request. I feel you are best suited for it and I hope you will oblige this old woman."

She took my hand. It was warm but weak and dry. Her pulse was surprisingly strong.

"I want to tell you my life story. Everything. From my girlhood in Germany to my *aliyah*. I want you to put it down in writing. You write stories. I want you to write mine. I would be honored if you would."

I had probably told her of my interest in hearing stories from my father and his friends who gathered most mornings at a seafront cafe and held court. Every visit to Bertha brought more curiosity about her life but there were boundaries. Now she was issuing my passport and opening the gate.

"The story is long and involved. Many people. Some good, others...." She waved her hand dismissively. "Many parts are unpleasant. You must know that from your father and his friends. You have some idea of what the war years were like."

I nodded.

"I leave it all in your hands. Only you and Nadia will know. After I go, you may do with your writings what you will. It's entirely up to you."

So her name was Nadia. She looked sad, of course, but also sheepish. She stood and left, saying only that she would return in a while.

"Bertha, my dearest Bertha, I'll be pleased and honored to hear of your life and put it down into words as best I can. These stories

5

are important to me. They should be so to everyone but that's less the case now."

"So true, so true. It's settled then. Out you go, young man. Come back tomorrow with pen and paper or whatever you writers use these days and we'll begin. We need to get started right away. Just you and me. Nadia will be fine."

She looked out the window and saw a bus come to a halt and let a few passengers out.

I arrived shortly after nine am. No pad of paper. A recording device. Not a digital one, a perfectly serviceable cassette deck.

"Sit! Sit, young man! We have work to do. So much work to do! I hope you brought lunch."

I held up a paper bag.

MUNICH

I was about ten years old when I first noticed it. It caught me completely off guard. My friend Anna and I had just completed our last class of the day and were preparing to walk the two kilometers to our homes. Anna had other plans.

"I'm waiting for my mom. We are going downtown to buy a new dress. For me!"

"What kind of dress?" I asked as we collected our books.

"Bertha! Such a forgetful one! I told you not more than a few days ago about it. I am going to get the white dress with the blue ribbons that was in a store window on Kaufingerstraße. Oh, I can't wait! I just can't wait!"

"Oh, yes. Yes, you did tell me. So much schoolwork."

I glanced at Anna and felt a sudden feeling of profound dread. I'd experienced nothing like it before. I busied myself with packing books and planning homework but the feeling persisted. Indeed, it worsened and caused my heart to race and perspiration to form on my forehead. Anna remained cheerful and eager to meet her mother for the big shopping spree.

"It's at Mr. Menuhin's store."

I suddenly became certain that tragedy was upon her. The joy I saw in Anna's face would soon enough be swept away and replaced with sorrow. Her mother would not meet her in front of the school and there would be no trip to Kaufingerstraße. Poor Anna would never see her again. The thought sank from my heart to my stomach and I felt nauseous as though from sailing a small boat on a lake as a storm came upon me.

"Are you well, Bertha?"

"Yes, thank you. I am fine. Too much schoolwork, I suppose. I'll be fine. The walk home will do me well."

"Oh, Bertha! Will you come over tonight? I'd love it if you helped me try the dress on and we all know hems need to be taken in or out on new clothing."

Dread and cause returned with greater force. I looked to my best friend and could fight it no longer. I kneeled down and began to spit up.

"Bertha! Shall I call Frau Feldman?"

"No, no, I'll be fine. You go with your mother. I must go to the bathroom to clean up before walking home. I'll see you soon, Anna." I paused for a second. I wanted to tell her but I couldn't. How would I explain this feeling to her? How could I destroy her hopes and dreams?

I ran to the restroom.

After calming myself and freshening up, I looked outside to the school entrance and saw Anna's father holding her hand as he led her to the family's automobile. Anna looked back to the school and saw me. Her eyes told the story. No shopping with mother again.

The next day my mother told me that Anna's mother had suffered a heart attack while carrying coal upstairs. I felt terrible for my friend and cursed by the foreknowledge. I wondered if my thoughts had caused her mother's death, though I recognized I saw things to come and did not bring them about. That came to me upon reflection. It was clear.

There was nothing in my background to lead me in the direction of extraordinary perceptiveness. I was born in 1909, the only child of Abraham and Sonia Siegelman of Munich. Father was a professor of mathematics at the University of Munich and mother taught piano at the conservatory. Numbers and notes, equations and concertos.

Their positions allowed us to live quite comfortably in a district where doctors, lawyers, and prosperous merchants lived in large dwellings built in the early part of the century. Trees that were saplings then now gave shade and ambiance.

We were Jewish but not especially religious. That was quite common in Germany between the wars. We observed the high holy days, enjoyed Shabbat dinners, and walked to synagogue, though I confess our attendance was spotty even with good weather. Father used to say he was a man of science and logic, yet we cannot ignore our ancestry and roots. They were part of who we were and to lose them was to become a leaf in the wind.

My parents doted on me, as did all four grandparents who lived in Munich as well. My every wish was granted. Most of them anyway. Holidays, religious and secular, brought an abundance of gifts – toys, shoes, dresses – so many I didn't know what to do with them all. No one would say I was deprived of anything, material or emotional, but no one would say it brought conceit either. In other words, I wasn't what we might call a brat. Family comfort brought trust, confidence, and a sense of belonging.

Not long after the incident with Anna at school I began to take notice of certain thoughts and feelings. I would sometimes feel a sense of being in an ocean, not in danger, but in harmony – and in boundless oneness. I sensed things were going to happen. Nothing extraordinary, at least not at first. Simple things like what mother would cook for dinner on a certain day or the unexpected arrival of an uncle. I'd mention events in the past, either regarding our extended family or something in Munich's history, and my parents would wonder how I knew of them. Perhaps I'd overheard my parents speak of them but if so, they had no recollection of it. We let it go at that. Just something I heard a relative say while I was a toddler.

I knew what my test scores would be and those of many classmates. An unexpected change in weather was seen well in advance. I'd hold a friend's hand or look into her eyes and sense a misfortune had recently befallen her or a pleasant surprise was in store.

I once sensed that a neighbor was doing bad things to a girl in my school – things that I couldn't comprehend then but that were well enough known to adults, even then. I sensed her shame and pain, fear and helplessness. The bad things would continue to happen and I felt her emotions as though they were echoing off a wall and reaching my soul.

I kept it all inside. No, not entirely. I told Anna several weeks after her mother's heart attack, and I continued to share a few thought I'd had after immersing myself in that feeling. Two young girls shared a secret, and kept it too. But I gathered the courage to tell my mother of my suspicions. Believing my friend had confided in me, my mother talked with my friend's parents.

Children were not told of such things but I envisioned police meeting with the girl and learning dreadful, sickening details. In a few weeks my friend was more cheerful, though there were scars deep down.

There were too many of such experiences. It was nothing I mentioned to anyone or tried to take advantage of. It was unpleasant, unsettling, mysterious, and foreboding. When I held a schoolmate's hand I wanted to feel love and trust, not sense her past and future. I just wanted to be a little girl. Nonetheless, this gift was with me. It was an essential part of who I was.

Secrets do not last long with young people. Either the joy bursts forth or the unease calls for help. When I was sixteen I could contain it no longer. I had to tell my father. It was a Saturday as my father, a man of science and logic, and I were walking to the synagogue. It was autumn and colorful leaves had fallen on the sidewalk and the air was crisp. We passed grocers and bakeries closed for the Sabbath.

"I have something important to tell you, father."

"What is it, my precious one?"

"It's about something I've felt, something I've known, for some time."

Father stopped and turned to me in alarm.

"Does this have something to do with a boy at school?"

"No, no. Nothing at all like that. It goes back many years, ever since I was a little girl. For some reason that I cannot explain, I know about things before they happen."

"Well, you are perceptive and make valid inferences. In my field of mathematics we calculate probabilities and make predictions, albeit tentatively at times. We Siegelmans are smart people. I've told you that many times and given you many opportunities to see it for yourself!"

"Indeed you have, father. What I do is not a logical calculation. I don't find probabilities. I just *know* things. Things about the past I've never heard of. Things about the future that cannot be known by ordinary methods."

"These are just gut feelings, my dear Bertha. Intuitions mixed with hopes. We all have them and we think they have merit but if we apply statistical methods to them, we soon learn they have no validity. When we're right, we remember it well. When we're wrong, ach, we forget it. The statistics are clear on this, Bertha."

"I knew that Anna's mother died before any word had come."

"One feeling out of hundreds."

"And I know that Rabbi Schneider is sick today and his replacement will be Rabbi Mayer."

My father hesitated. He knew nothing of the matter and couldn't think of any way I could have.

"Well, let's just see."

And with that, we ascended the steps and entered the neo-Roman synagogue where we'd long attended services and where the boys had had their Bar Mitzvahs. We sat and father looked about for Rabbi Schneider.

"He's not here, father. I *know* it."

Rabbi Mayer soon enough stood before the assembly and announced that Rabbi Schneider was ill and that he would be conducting the service that evening. Father looked over to me briefly but said nothing. I was too young and respectful to respond with an "I told you so look." Besides, I felt uneasy about the whole thing.

All the way back home I told my father of other instances of seeing ahead but a math professor doesn't abandon his ideas easily.

He went on and on about alternate explanations. As we neared home, where we knew mother would have a meal of some sort prepared, I whispered, "Father! You're in for a delight! Mother has made us a wonderful brunch of potatoes, strawberry blintzes, and fried eggs!"

"Well, that would be different, Bertha. Whatever it is, I shall demonstrate an uncanny ability to make it vanish."

"By eating it!"

"Just so, young lady. Just so. But I may need your help."

We sat at the table and in a trice mother came from the kitchen with a serving tray covered with a damask napkin. She placed it on the table and pulled away the napkin.

"Voila! A spectacular repast for my loved ones. Potatoes, blintzes and fried eggs."

Father briefly glanced at me. "Sonia! I am both grateful and amazed. But what kind of blintzes?"

I broke with tradition for children at the table and sliced a blintz in two.

"They're strawberry, father! Of course!"

The math professor gave me another glance, this time with less assurance. Something wasn't adding up, so to speak.

That night, my father knocked on my door. He sat on the bed and released a long sigh.

"Sweet one, you know that I am a man of science and have been since I was your age. I can't accept things if they are not supported by scientifically-established studies. Honestly, what I saw today astonished me. I am not sure how you do it. Not sure at all. But I want you to know something. This, this gift must be kept secret. If it's known by outsiders... well, there will be problems. Some people will insist that you help them. Others will think you have dark powers and there are too many such legends around our people already. This must stay inside the doors of our house."

"Yes, father. Of course. I have already suspected that it could cause trouble, yet sometimes I think I can help people choose a better path or avoid a bad one."

"Well, that's the problem I have with the phenomenon, my dear. We can't really change the future by knowing what's going to happen. This is a rule of logic. We would create a paradox. Letting people know about future events may cause them harm. The world has its reasons why we can't see the future. It's for our own good. For example, I don't want to know the day of my death. I know it will come but foreknowledge would cause anxiety and maybe rashness."

"Of course, father. We can't change the past because it's already set, but we can change what has not happened yet. Can't we?"

"I don't think so. What is meant to happen, will happen. That's nature. Others would say it's God's will. We cannot change it. It will happen in one way or another."

"We can have a certain knowledge of the future and prepare for it. We know that winter is coming by our calendar and we prepare our homes and clothing for the cold weather. That doesn't change the weather or the future but it changes what we do for the future."

For the first time my father struggled with ideas he had not mastered. His gears were turning but slowly and uneasily. He simply couldn't explain the phenomenon scientifically or know what to do with it. Well, neither did I. Who did?

"Bertha, I can't answer you as I don't have the scientific evidence at hand to formulate an answer. I doubt I ever will. For your own good. Keep your gift a secret. Give me your word on that."

"I promise, father. You have my word."

That was the first time I gave my word to anyone. Unfortunately, years later I broke that promise. I had to in order to survive.

Not long thereafter we visited my mother's mother who lived only a short drive from our home. Grandma Rivka as I called her was eighty-one years old but retained a free-spirited soul and was as lovable as any grandmother in a storybook. A diminutive woman with white hair and folds that conveyed intelligence and experience, she lived alone in small house since her husband died when I was about ten. My parents wanted her to live in our house. There was enough room. She would cheerfully decline, insisting she could make do by herself.

Naturally, she was delighted to hear of our visit and greeted us in the late morning as our car came noisily down the stone road. She stopped watering the plants on the front porch and scurried inside to the kitchen. Rugelach and coffee for the folks, the same pastry for me but with hot chocolate. She was glad to see her daughter and son-in-law but I felt my presence delighted her the most.

Later, she and I walked about the town and sat in park, chatting, feeding pigeons, and simply enjoying life. Vendors sold grilled chestnuts on the spot. The walks usually ended with a stop at a sweets shop before heading home, which I loved tremendously.

"Grandma, I want to tell you a secret."

"Of course, dear. Is it about a boy in your class? Those are my favorite secrets and have been since I was your age in the days of the Kaisers!"

"No, no. It is something totally different. I promised father I'd never tell anyone, but I simply have to tell someone. I want tell you. I have no secrets from you. Promise not to tell it to anyone."

"I promise."

"Grandma, I…"

She suddenly put a finger to her lips.

"Shhh, dear. Don't speak of it. It isn't good. Nor is it necessary. I already know what you want to tell me. As you said, you and I have no secrets. Bertha. my dearest, you have the gift."

Her blue eyes sparkled with her smile and I recognized something in her for the first time. I thought of my friend Anna and her mother.

"You have the wonderful gift. I saw it in you before you did. You were quite young, only two or three. I looked in you and saw it – or felt it. We know some things before they happen. You've sensed it for quite some time. Your schoolmate and her tragedy sealed the notion in your mind. My gift is not as keen as it once was. Today, oh…today the future no longer has the allure it once had. The final event is coming. Anyone can see that. Your gift, however, is just beginning. It will grow stronger with time – and with practice."

"I know it will, grandma."

She saw my concern and anxiety and inability to express myself.

"Have no fear. It is a good thing and it will be of help. You cannot use it frivolously. It must be used sparingly and wisely. Save it. Guard it. Treasure it. One day it will prove invaluable."

I carefully watched her aged face as she gave me a loving smile. I loved her so much.

We stopped a short way from her home and she pressed me to her heart. A sense of oceanic oneness came over me and I let it sweep over us like warm soothing waters. Then there was something else. My heart sunk. All of a sudden I knew. I fought my tears.

"Grandma! Grandma, you are not well!"

She took my hand as we continued home.

"Yes, yes. It's true. You're quite right. The hour is late, my child, and the shadows long. I've been blessed with a wonderful life, a loving husband, a beautiful daughter, and a sweet granddaughter whom I love so much. Great things lie ahead for you, Bertha. What else could anyone ask for?"

"No one knows but us?"

"They will know when the time comes. No need to worry them now. It will be difficult but the world will continue on its way. Days pass, years come around." A brief moment of dread came across us. "You must be careful with your gift, dear Bertha. Bad people, evil people, will want to use it for their ends and you must never let them."

"You will always be with me, grandma. Ever in my heart." I couldn't hold back tears anymore and I threw myself into her embrace.

"Always, dear, always. But, Bertha, evil is coming and you must prepare for it."

I didn't know what she meant but her words stayed with me.

We returned home and enjoyed dinner and a radio broadcast from an immense wooden console in the living room with glowing tubes. As we prepared to leave for Munich I kissed my grandmother goodbye. We knew it was our last time together and treasured every moment. I gave her a long hug as she smiled and nodded goodbye. Her eyes told me everything.

Word came from a neighbor but a few days later. A gentle woman had passed away peacefully at home in her sleep.

It was the conversation with grandma that made me appreciate my privilege and not allow it to pick away at me with delusions and whims, pettiness, and rages. I kept my word to her and my father. I nurtured my gift an practiced it, though in secret. It was fun to have perceptions that others couldn't dream of. For an unknown reason that I did not understand, I had the gift. And for some equally unknown reason I had to use it wisely and benevolently. For whom and when I could not know though I knew some dread events were coming.

I graduated from *gymnasium* with honors in 1927 and in the autumn became a history student at the University of Munich. The subject had interested me at *gymnasium* and there was so much going on in the country then. The monarchy had fallen at the end of the world war in 1918 and a democracy was in Berlin. After the inflation was stanched in the early twenties, the economy thrived and the arts flourished. A new day was dawning. I'd read of great figures such as Pericles, Rousseau, and Hugo and garnered insights as to how they thought and shaped their times. I even had thoughts about how they courted and loved. It was such fun for a gifted young woman!

Father and mother were not pleased by my choice of history. Father found the study impractical. Better to study chemistry, engineering, biology, or mathematics. They knew I loved history and it was reflected during my university years in my grades and praise from teachers, so they never tried to steer me away. The stolid professors in their robes and mortarboards were so kind and unbound by the academy's conventions regarding women that they encouraged me to go on to graduate work and get an appointment in the Munich faculty.

Early modern history was my specialty, though Ancient Rome and the Kingdom of Israel attracted me as well. Great civilizations came and went, armies marched and battled, treaties were signed and dishonored. The dynamics were fascinating.

I also met the love of my life while at university. It was the first semester of my sophomore year in a comparative religion class. The professor posed a question to the class regarding Passover, which in the context of the lecture was its relationship to Good Friday and Easter. Remember, Jews were not well represented in the student body back then. A young man quickly raised his and when called upon, delivered a concise, respectful account of the famed occasion. I was charmed by his eloquent and obvious but understated passion. His attire and dark hair were less than tidy which made him even more boyish looking.

Finishing his reply and retaking his seat, he looked around the class, gauging reactions. Or maybe he was just looking at me! Either way, our eyes met and oh, there was something there! Something striking and unexpected and wonderful. It was only after a few moments did I return to the lecture on Julius Wellhausen. I summoned my gift. I had to. What did this exchange of glances portend? I drifted into the oceanic realm and waited for sensations to come over me. Moments passed, many of them, but nothing came to me. I was baffled and not a little annoyed. Back to the Julius Wellhausen lecture.

Happily, there was always the more routine approach: having a meal with him. We saw each other at the university commissary and I was delighted when he came over to my table.

"Well, hello. My name is Joshua Rosen and I believe we are in the same comparative religion class."

Such eyes, such a smile, such a young man!

"Yes, we are. I'm Bertha Siegelman. And you are a most eloquent speaker."

"And you are a most beautiful young woman."

"A shopworn phrase that you've used often, I'm sure."

"I confess you're correct. This time, I truly mean it."

"Judging by your way of dressing, Joshua, you aren't Orthodox."

"Quite observant, so to speak! My parents are quite strict and I was raised that way but in recent years I've adopted a more open life. And you, Bertha?"

"My family observes the high holy days but attendance at *schul* is not flawless shall we say. I loved your brief representation in class the other day!"

Again, our eyes met and bored into each other's souls. Something was coming, anyone could know that. Joshua leaned over and gently kissed me on the lips. This wasn't done in Germany back then, except perhaps in Berlin cabarets and then only after several drinks. It simply wasn't done – but it was simply amazing and lasting. We saw each other every day and went out together on Saturday nights.

A few months later we made the bold step of living together in a small apartment a ten-minute walk from the university. That simply wasn't done either. A couple had to be married before they shared a dwelling. My parents were dismayed and I'm sure his were all the more so but this was the Weimar period and norms had been easing for years. My parents asked every few weeks when Joshua and I would tie the knot but I gently put them off. When it happens, it happens.

After a few months it indeed happened. It was a small ceremony attended by only a dozen people and conducted by a recently dismissed judge my father knew from school. The paperwork was never filed as that would put us on another list for some watchful wretch to study one day.

The apartment was a wonderful place to start out. We'd buy a small Persian rug or a clock from a second-hand shop and feel our home become warmer. The balcony looked out on a park where children played in warmer months and snow covered the grass in the winter. I can still see flecks of snow slanting down in the yellow glow of gas lights.

My gift was inexplicably of no use on the matter of stomping the glass. In fact, I was able to discern nothing of our future. Instead of an omen it was a mystery, another dimension of the exploration of our love. We had to go ahead blind, just as everyone else does!

This added more mystery to him in my view. In a few years I'd become a *privatdozent* – a lecturer for undergrads. Joshua, two years my junior, continued his studies and helped make ends meet by working in a bicycle shop. Neither job put us in the chips but we fared well enough and looked forward to a wonderful life together.

THE WIND

My gift was largely dormant, especially when I was in Joshua's arms. That didn't bother me. I never even told him about it. We simply went about lives. It was puzzling yet welcome as the gift had always been at least somewhat of a burden, something that set me off from the rest of the world. My world was now our apartment overlooking the park and teaching history.

Quite late one spring night, as we sat on the balcony, Joshua was sound asleep and I drowsed. I began to shiver and became wary. I felt in mid-ocean again. My gift was returning. I sensed dread, looked to the night sky, and braced myself for a wave of thoughts and feelings. I knew they would not be good. Clouds covered the gibbous moon and few stars are in sight. I felt cold and vulnerable. Evil was at hand and it would grab hold of all of us, not just Joshua and me and out loved ones, this evil would plague the world.

Yes, Hitler had become chancellor a few weeks earlier but I wasn't overly concerned by that and my gift let the day pass without incident. Now it was in full force, telling me of complacency and coming disaster, not only for Joshua and me.

Over the next few years one horrible event followed another. Hitler and his gang used a clause in the constitution to take complete control. Antisemitism took on the force of law. Governmental machinery went to work. Jewish shops were marked, then attacked. It wasn't safe for us to walk down streets, though our attire was hardly traditional. The number of Jewish students was limited and Jews were banned from many professions.

When that grim process began, we knew it would continue. My father, Joshua, and I knew our university positions were in danger.

Word came soon. My *privatdozent* position was terminated. When I asked the reason, I was told it was government policy. Everything had been done orderly, officially, and despicably. My father's dismissal came the same day, though I didn't hear of it until that night. Many thought the Nazi policies would be rolled back at some point, a year or so. The German people were too smart and decent to accept this resurfacing of medieval blood hate. My feelings were the opposite. We were just entering a very dark period that would last many years and cost many lives.

Ah, my gift. I never mentioned it to my husband. Not even that spring night, not even as mobs broke the windows of Jewish shops. I respected the wishes of my grandmother and father. I confess, however, that Joshua would think his wife was a little *meshuggeneh*, at least for a long while.

Joshua lost his job at the bicycle shop. Even that position required pure Aryan blood. It was hard to make ends meet and we considered moving out of the city, but we didn't want to leave our families. They owned houses and were reluctant to give them up.

Anna, my old schoolmate, visited me! It was an absolute delight to see her again. We sat on the balcony overlooking the park and talked, mostly about our school days but it was only a matter of time until the present would be brought up.

"Times are hard for us, Anna. Joshua and I cannot find work."

"It's the same with us. It's the same for all of us, I'm afraid. We're living on savings and we are not the Rothschilds."

"Nor are we. Our savings are near the end and we're looking for ways to make a little money. That Persian rug in the parlor? We love it but we may have to sell it."

"Bertha, someone like you can earn money. You know – with that special talent."

"You had to bring that up! Yes, I told you of it and it's been our treasured secret. Only you and my parents know of it and I promised I'd not divulge it."

"I understand that completely but with the dreadfulness and uncertainty that's upon us we have to eke out livings somehow. We have to whatever we can to keep body and soul together. Furthermore, the uncertainty makes people search for hope and for some idea of what lies ahead. People will flock to you, Bertha."

"I see the fear on people's faces on the streets. You're right. But who will pay money to hear a soothsayer, a fortunetelle? Besides, the Reich isn't fond of Gypsies either."

"Oh Bertha! I know several people who desperately want to find out what's in store for us. They try to read tea leaves and look to the sky for signs."

"What if what I see ahead for them isn't good?"

"Ach…. You'll have to use your judgment there, dear. Promise me you will keep this in mind."

"I will."

Hard times became harder for Joshua and me. We sold the rug and that helped for a while but a few weeks later we were down to rye bread and boiled cabbage. Every day, rye and cabbage. I met Anna at the marketplace and told her I'd changed my mind.

For the next few days, I tried to get into shape, so to speak. I stood next to people in groceries and bakeries, then closed my eyes for impressions to come over me. I did this for several weeks and soon felt ready. Back home I closed the drapes, set up a few candles, and placed a small table in the center of our parlor. With Joshua out for the evening, I was ready for my first client.

A young woman named Maria knocked tentatively at the door. I greeted her and bade her to come in. She was about my age and greatly troubled. It was clear from her face and hesitant speech and the way she held her arms close in. I was tense and that wasn't helpful. I had to chat with her a while to put us both at ease, then I began breathing in and out methodically until I felt the sea around me. I'd seen her look of dismay the moment I opened the door. Now I felt her troubles – no, her anguish and despair. I took her hand and her soul burst forth into mine. I almost wept as our souls merged for a few terrible moments.

"Your husband…." I hesitated briefly. "It's him. Franz. He's being unfaithful… with a close friend… a close friend of yours."

"Oh my! You know my husband's name! What of my friend, his lover? I have to know!"

"Her name is Rosa."

"How could you have known. How could you have known but for…."

"The affair has been going on some time. Perhaps a year."

"Where? Where do they meet?" The poor woman was sobbing and pleading.

"He works in a building in the city center, she in a small shop not far away. They have trysts in her apartment above the shop. Noontimes. Often, very often. A flower shop. That's where she works. I can see it better. But… Rosa is married and has a child."

"Oh my! Oh my! What about her husband? And they have a child. Does he know?"

A wave came over me, one more unpleasant than the previous ones and I hesitated. I opened my eyes. "Maybe you should talk this over with Franz. There is only so much I can see."

"No, I want to know! Please, I must know!"

Her pleading would not allow me to end things then, though it was best we did.

"My dear Maria, I'm afraid I have to tell you that your husband is the father of Rosa's boy. I am truly sorry. I wish it were not so. Bertha's word."

She sobbed openly for several minutes before composing herself and reaching into her purse for a generous amount of Reichsmarks. I never saw her again. I felt awful. Giving people bad news is never pleasant but Anna told me that Maria had left her husband and was now living with a friend. The Reichsmarks served a purpose yet I felt sadness for her. It took some time for me to accept the fact that ultimately knowing the truth, as much as it hurts, is better than living the lie.

Anna sent me another client, a young man who was a middle manager at a manufacturing firm in Munich. Tall and meticulous, and not one to put anyone at ease. Maria was troubled but in a way that elicited sympathy. This fellow conveyed darkness.

"Please, give me your hands and we can begin."

More darkness. I felt danger, not for me though. Otherwise, I'd have called the session off, saying I felt nothing. No fee.

"You have resentments at your workplace. A man above you, a Herr Kahan."

A slight smile came across his face and he nodded,

"He will soon be let go. He is a Jew. And this pleases you. You are certain that you will be promoted to his post."

"I am impressed. Truly so. Would that it be so for all those *Untermenschen*."

"You are happy... that he will be fired because he is a Jew... and you'll get his job."

I pulled my hands back, not because of his words though.

"Continue. I insist."

"You reported bad things about him to the Gestapo. False things. You lied to them."

"Well, yes I did. He and his ilk have been sapping the strength of our nation too long. Yes, yes, I know of his family but they have money. Those people roll in it."

He was giving me a lecture, one I'd heard too often. He must have thought I was a Gypsy, though he was unlikely to have enlightened views of them either. I wanted to return to the reading and conclude it as quickly as possible, though I confess I wanted his marks and perhaps even a return.

"Your plan will succeed. Kahan will be gone soon and you'll get his job. That's all I can say today. Bertha's word."

"Excellent news! You are amazing. I'll pass the word to friends and coworkers."

He stood, reached into an inner pocket in his suit coat, and tossed down a roll of marks on the table. I was never so pleased to hear a door close and footfalls on the stairway, though more loathsome clients were to darken my door in coming years. I stared at the pile of marks until I heard him reach the ground floor and exit. Even then it took a few minutes before I counted the money. It was an unpleasant but lucrative deal transaction but we had to make a living. We had to buy food, pay the rent and bills. That's what kept me going.

Joshua still didn't know. Not about my gift, not about my new job. I'd have to tell him where the money came. Those two readings alone paid for food and rent to last over a month. I had no earthly idea how he'd take it.

"This is wonderful! Bertha, you are amazing! I wish you had told me earlier but this is no time for small matters. We can get by now!"

"I promised my family not to divulge my ability. Also, I was afraid of it. I still am. Knowing the future and having people rely on you can bring problems."

"All is well, my dear. We have a source of income now and we can see that it grows. Maybe I can help out as an assistant. We can decorate the salon in a more appealing way. A new rug!"

His judgment was clouded by elation over having money. Understandable, but I didn't quite like it.

"While I'm in a session with people, I feel many things. Some good, some not so good. In fact, I felt the presence of darkness in one man and he was part of a larger, dangerous darkness that hates us. It is an ugly place to be."

"Oh yes. I'm sure you're right. There will always be good and bad people in our world. We'll just have to learn to let them work with you without touching inside you. It's like being a doctor who treats all sorts of people, good and bad, without letting them affect him. They're in the office one minute, out the next. Keep your emotions away. It's just a job."

"The doctor doesn't feel the evil in people, not the way I do. Feeling people's inner beings isn't part of medical work. It's essential to my work – essential and unpleasant and maybe more. As the philosopher says, when you peer into evil, it peers into you."

He gave me a loving hug and I felt better. "It's only temporary until this madness is over. A few years. That's all."

He enjoyed a good meal for a change. The atmosphere became more cheerful and I was happy to put everything behind.

My work went on. I learned and became better at it. Aside from the spiritual perceptions there were ordinary signs. The most important one is that people don't want to hear bad news. A session that foretold misfortune led to misfortune for my household: one less customer and one less payment, at least. Good news or at least no bad news kept people coming. Nonetheless, I was not sparing in giving unwelcome readings.

I always ended sessions by saying, "Bertha's word." It became my signature and word spread. We hired a craftsman to create a sign with those two words in large gothic print and displayed it prominently in the reading room.

In less than a year I was giving ten to fifteen readings a week. I was famous, even though I made no display of crystal balls and Tarot cards. Everyone in Munich knew of me. We went from dire poverty to dizzying affluence, despite the Third Reich's shadow.

It was time to move out and up. We rented a larger apartment from an elderly woman who needed rent money while she lived with her daughter. We purchased another Persian rug, a Khamseh, to replace the one we had to sell.

Joshua doubled as accountant and mysterious man at the door who beckoned people in before disappearing. The trade continued to prosper, probably because the monsters in Berlin were causing so much anxiety. People felt more assured when I told them, as I almost always did, that everything was working out for the best. Those monsters saw that it wasn't. Many sessions gave me feelings of customers' futures that caused me to shudder and have nightmares.

I did not advertise myself around town as a Jewish mystic, practiced in Kabbalah. Nor did Joshua and I keep a menorah or other items of Judaica in prominent places. We kept them stored away in an armoire.

In early 1937 a knock came. A customer had told me he was referring an important acquaintance at this hour so Joshua hied to the door and brought him to the parlor, where I sat with welcoming countenance.

"Frau Bertha, I take it."

I hope that disposition did not fall away the instant I saw him but the energy I received from him was cold, official, military. He had the rugged handsomeness of propaganda art and I expected a sense of evil to come but it did not, despite an NSDAP pin on the lapel of his dark blue suit. It fit him smartly and suggested careful tailoring. He was soldier and part of the Reich machinery.

"Indeed, I am Frau Bertha. Please be seated. There's tea steeping in the pot."

"That would be most agreeable. I am Reinhard Beck."

We sat at the table in the salon with curtains drawn. Joshua poured tea for us before taking his routine leave. I took only a desultory sip or two before getting to the matter at hand.

"Why have you come to me, Herr Beck? Surely it wasn't for my tea."

"Many reasons, though your tea isn't one of them. Firstly, to determine if you have the power of clairvoyance. Tell me what you know of me."

He lit a cigarette and held it in one hand and presented the other to me. I was obliged to take hold of it. I let myself drift into the sea, half expecting to be struck by nauseating thoughts. He was vain and direct, a true believer in the cause, but there was something else quite surprising. I felt in charge. He was manipulable. In retrospect this was to be expected as his sort had already surrendered their will and accepted all orders from above. He might be highly useful. Another sensation came to me, a wholly unexpected one. Though devoted to the cause there was an underlying naïveté and decency.

"Herr Beck, I'll thank you to extinguish your cigarette and give me both hands. There is much energy for me to take in."

He complied at once and I went deeper into the sea.

"You have unmistakable power. You are in an elite formation. An officer. A promising one."

"Bravo, Frau Bertha! I am in the SS."

We knew of the SS and hated them. They had massacred scored of people in 1934 to seal Hitler's power and since then had been arresting dissidents, especially Jewish ones, and imprisoning them not far from Munich at a vast camp called Dachau.

"The SS is charged with enforcing the Reich's laws. Most notably the ones pertaining to Jews. Their property and businesses are seized."

As I spoke, I saw people beaten and humiliated. Beck seemed distant from this and his naïveté struck me again. He marched along confident in his righteousness. That is how I conceptualized the essence of Nazism in 1937. To some extent, despite what was to come, I still see it that way for many of the Reich's followers in and out of uniform.

Beatings and torture and graves as far as I could see. Trains with hundreds of cars churning through a green countryside that turned gray then black. The oceanic feeling was too much. I felt close to vomiting.

"What? What do you see, Frau Bertha?"

"I'm sorry. this reading has been very taxing on me. I'm exhausted and we must call it off for now and continue another time."

"No need to apologize. You have proven your merit to me. Can you please tell me one more thing? The SS is growing and I want to grow with it. Will I be promoted?"

I closed my eyes.

"Oh, yes. You will grow with the SS and rise in its ranks. Your promotion...later this year. Bertha's word. There will be a cost but it will not be borne by you. Worry not of that, Herr Beck. I must end the session now. Accordingly, I cannot ask for any payment."

"I won't hear of it! I am amazed and most grateful."

Joshua had gone shopping and made a point to delay his return until my session was over. When he opened the door, I rushed to his arms and trembled.

"Did it not go well?"

"It went too well. The Nazis will not fade away like the *pogromshiks* before them. They are growing in size and malevolence. They will destroy everything! They will kill everyone! There's no way out, Joshua! There's nowhere to flee to! All Europe, all Europe!"

We sat and finished the tea. I stared at Beck's half-empty cup. Joshua tried to calm me, saying nothing could be that bad and that I was exaggerating my visions and letting fear get the better of me. I persisted though and he reflected on conversations he had had with family and it all coalesced into a belief that a nightmare was upon us.

"Is that Beck fellow a danger to us?"

I thought over my mixed perceptions struggled to form a reply.

"He is dangerous. He will bring great harm. But he will be for help."

"Oh, Bertha, at times like this you baffle me. Nonetheless, I love you with all my heart."

We embraced and I felt a sense of distant dread.

"I love you too, Joshua. We shall have to face things together."

Germany was becoming more authoritarian and more antisemitic and more bent on war. You could sense it everywhere and did not need a gift to do so. The imminence of war exhilarated many people. It was a way to right wrongs and restore honor. I suppose all wars are like that early on.

My parents were no longer able to make ends meet and I gave them money. He spoke repeatedly of science and logic and how medieval and illogical thinking had taken hold. He said it so often that I thought he was falling into despair. But Jews were being harangued and beaten on the streets.

Inside my parlor, there was no slowdown. Customer after customer came for readings and I gave them my perceptions on things like love, careers, families. There were other things that I did not tell them of. I sensed a sense of joy and wellbeing from Germany coming back to greatness. Wages rose, shops prospered, people walked the streets with purpose. The nation, they felt, was in good hands and though there were occasional excesses, well so be it. They had previously had Jewish friends but now they saw them as non-Germans. More importantly, they saw them as responsible for the wrongs of the past. Looking into my clients' hearts I saw the Reich's ideology pervaded them and they accepted it almost entirely.

We had to wear the Star of David on our clothing. And Jewish stores were ransacked on Kristallnacht. The police stood by as SS paramilitary and "ordinary" people broke shop windows, looted, and burned. Synagogues too. Precious scrolls and ancient artifacts were stolen or destroyed. It wasn't safe to walk the streets. The past with all its comforts and hopes was collapsing along with law and order and human dignity.

I began reading the newspapers more diligently. There were accounts of smiling policemen and firemen standing by as people were beaten and property destroyed. It wasn't just in Munich, it was all across Germany and Austria, which had been integrated with the Third Reich. Some 25,000 Jews were rounded up, beaten, and sent to detainment centers – what we would later call "concentration camps." Hitler and his machinery were threatening to annihilate the Jews.

We had already hidden our Judaica from our home but now we put them at my parents or in storage. We couldn't bring ourselves to throw them away or sell them. Abandoning who were would have been dishonorable.

Business went on. I worried that word would spread that I was a Jew, though I'd shown no sign of that for years. At that horrid time I would have been branded not only an *Untermensch* but also a witch. What would a mob have done to me? Most clients came and went without incident. We had enough money to bribe our way out of Germany and settle in Switzerland but our parents insisted on staying and Joshua and I could not leave them.

Late in 1938 Herr Beck came for another reading. It was his fourth or fifth, most of which were ordinary foretelling of his career prospects. Those readings had been scheduled. That day he simply showed up and demanded my time. It was clear that he knew I was Jewish and that disarmed me. I no longer had mastery over him, though I knew he still had vulnerabilities. I took his hands and immersed myself in the sea. Great evil washed over me, though oddly not from him personally. I had to calm myself nonetheless.

"What do you see, Frau Bertha? I know you see something. I do not have your powers but I know you are feeling something right now. Tell me what it is. I insist."

"Your organization respects you and has bigger things planned for you."

"Here in Munich?"

"No, not in Munich. You will be promoted and ordered to a new posting. A large bureau. A secretive one with many, many people."

"That is excellent news! Munich is, well, a bit confining for a man like me. Bigger things are out there and I want to be part of them. Please tell me more. I know you see more."

He patted an inner coat pocket where he kept his folding money. He was a domineering man and accustomed to having his way.

"There will be many people there...."

"Yes, you said that."

"They will watch over the Reich...know everything going on... and look for foreign dangers. You will prosper there. You will know of things few people do, even the men in the chancellory."

"Yes! The Abwehr! Counterintelligence! The nation will be at war soon and enemies will abound."

"Four markers on your collar. You will be lauded in Berlin."

"Four markers! *Sturmbannführer* Beck!"

"Yes, that is it. You will be a Sturmbannführer."

"Amazing! I knew it. I felt it coming and talked about with fellow officers at the mess hall but now I know it to be true! There is just one more thing."

"And what might that be?"

"Your magical words!"

"Ah, yes. All that I said will happen, will indeed come to pass. Bertha's word."

"Bertha's word! Yes, there it is! Bertha's word!"

Beck reached into his coat pocket and peeled off an exceptionally larger number of bills.

"Is there something else? You look pensive, Frau Bertha."

I looked at him and felt his naïveté once more and saw how that would paradoxically help him in his new position in the Abwehr.

"No. Nothing. It was just a very taxing reading. That's all. The Reich is fortunate to have men like you."

He tossed down another bill and bade me goodbye. I was certain that he knew I was Jewish yet I also felt he would become a benefactor. O life! You can be so baffling.

THE CAMP

Beck came to see me every few months, as often as not in SS uniform. They no longer wore black as in their early years. The tunics and trousers were green. However, the skull and lightning insignia remained and so did the lawlessness and murderousness.

"Frau Bertha! You see before you a newly promoted man. But you knew of it before I did and even before Berlin did! Amazing! Wonderful! How you have set my mind at ease and directed me on the proper path to serve the Fatherland."

"Ahh. So I have played a part. Only a small one, I'm sure."

"Oh, my abilities were most important. And of course my ability to inspire those around me. I am inspecting a new facility north of here called Buchenwald. You have heard of it, no?"

"Yes, I have. It lies about a hundred kilometers southwest of Berlin."

"Correct! We have many thousands of prisoners there – criminals, spies, and the like. Oh yes. I neglected to mention that there are thousands of Jews there as well but am more concerned with political prisoners."

He gauged my reaction and I hoped I hid it. He paused long and hard, increasing my discomfort.

"Priceless! The expression on your face is absolutely priceless! Frau Bertha, I may not have your gift or your intelligence but even I know you are a Jew."

I could not have hidden anything just then, except for my fear of becoming a guest at Buchenwald.

"There, there, Bertha. Oh, let us dispense with the Frau and Herr nonsense. I mean you no harm. Your secret is safe with me. You help me and I help you. That's only fair. Ah, but we were talking of Buchenwald. Many thousands of inmates are there and we put them to work for the Reich. They work hard. Very hard. We see to that. They make military hardware, just as you foretold lo these many months. Well, the regimen is quite harsh. I suppose word gets out. Even I see it as unnecessarily so. But it is all for the good of Germany."

A true believer in the Reich. He was a cheerful young man, capable of admitting there was cruelty. His faith in the Reich helped him minimize it and overlook it. That was essential to the Nazi period. Too many people saw a higher end hovering beneficently over the evil means. Yes, Germany had too many people like him, though I would later think the country had far too few of them.

"Bertha, I am only in Munich for a short visit, official and otherwise. I have a train to catch. I will return periodically. And fret not. You are well cared for as long as Reinhard Beck holds sway over the Munich authorities. The Abwehr to them is a mysterious force and like to keep them stewing in that concern!"

And then he was off. Back to Buchenwald. Back to Berlin. Back to oiling the machinery that was grinding away on the world. It was 1939 and another war was coming.

Joshua and I spoke of Beck, Buchenwald, and the deteriorating situation. Beck was a true believer in the Reich and paradoxically, in me as well. There was no question where his ultimate loyalty lay but he still might be helpful to my husband and me, until he had to make the choice, if he ever did.

Many Jews were leaving Germany, many others thought Nazism would extinguish itself in a year or two. We visited my parents over the weekend and for the first time my father was recommending that Joshua and I get out. He had a house and considerable property but we could pack what we could, leave our apartment, and head to a safer place, though he did not know just where that was. Czechoslovakia had already been seized. Troops were massing near the border with Poland and invasion would mean a full European conflagration.

I agreed and told him that my sense was that darkness would fall soon and hard and that we should all leave. Nevertheless, my parents were adamant. They had a beautiful home filled with many heirlooms. Some items like their Kas armoire and desk were too large to take along and too dear to sell off. Joshua's parents were of the same view.

So, it was up to Joshua and me. Leave four parents behind or stay and face what was coming. The decision was not hard. We would stay in Munich, where National Socialism had begun. The descent continued, and there were remarkable steps on the way down.

THE
REICHSMARSCHALL

I t was at the end of August when Reinhard Beck paid me another visit – again unannounced. I couldn't very well tell him I was busy and close the door on him. It was late at night, about 11pm. Joshua headed for the bedroom and stayed quiet. Another man in an expensive black suit and overcoat accompanied Beck. I felt weakness and sickness the instant the two entered. The source was not Beck.

The companion was a stout man with a determined, hawk-like face, softened somewhat by a plump build. He looked familiar. It was like a moment seeing someone on the street and thinking you know them, then after a moment you realize it is a celebrity of one type or another. This was no actor, not in the usual sense. He wore a *Pour le Merite* device on his lapel.

"Bertha, old friend! Our paths meet once again. This time I have the pleasure of bringing a distinguished figure. I have apprised him of your talents and he was so intrigued that he insisted on meeting you himself."

The guest nodded amicably and smiled in a manner that conveyed superiority rather than friendship. Oh no, I thought. I knew who he was from the newspapers. I'd heard him speak on radio broadcasts from Berlin.

"It is my honor, dear Bertha, to introduce Generalfeldmarschall Hermann Göring. He is second only to our Führer, Adolf Hitler."

I could readily feel Göring's coarse soul. He thrived on power and authority. Yes, he is definitely a military being, yet also careless and selfish. I wondered if he could be useful to my family.

"Ah, Frau Bertha. Bertha if I may. Your reputation is notable. Reinhard here attests to that."

"I am most honored, gentlemen. May I suggest we take seats in the parlor?"

Göring removed his overcoat, revealing his considerable girth, and draped it over the chair. I lit candles and we sat at the table in the properly darkened room. Just as I was about to say a few words by way of getting to business, Göring spoke.

"The Reich is about to embark on a most ambitious effort, one that will right wrongs and restore the Fatherland to its former greatness. Naturally, there are uncertainties and naturally there are questions. Helpful answers will guide me and others in Berlin. And helpful answers will assure our continued willingness to exempt you from certain policies."

"The Jewish laws," Beck added – quite needlessly.

Göring presented his hands to me.

"That will not be necessary, good sir. Someone as formidable as yourself fairly radiates all I need to perceive."

I paused to calm myself. They thought I was deep in thought but it took time to reach the oceanic state. I saw an infant.

"It is always heartening to meet someone for whom the family is paramount. There is a newborn in your life."

"Edda. My daughter is named Edda. She is one year old."

He smiled but cautiously. After all, the information was probably in the Munich newspapers.

"You are a devoted family man and –"

He stood immediately and hovered over me.

"I am not especially devoted to my wife and offspring and I did not come here for trifling matters about family, horse races, and the weather next week."

His voice was deliberate, as though correcting an impertinent junior officer. His hand came in my direction and I braced myself. It came to rest on my breasts and I shuddered, perceptibly I'm sure.

"Frau Siegelman, we know who you are and above all what you are. We know of your parents and in-laws and if their dwellings and former places of work. We have records. Now, I need to know from you – and this very night – what the coming months will bring. Not for me, but for the Reich. As I said, we are beginning a bid to restore greatness and I must know what you see. And you must know that this is not a request or a business transaction. You are dealing with the *Reich*."

I struggled to return to the oceanic realm. It was easier when the lout removed his paw from my blouse. Perceptions came. Vivid ones. They dismayed me but they undoubtedly stirred warmth in him.

"There are trucks, tanks, planes, and men. Many, many of each. In the east. Large encampments, detailed plans. They are prepared, eager, willing. Victory will come."

"That I know! How quickly?"

"Events underway cannot be stopped. It will proceed well – and quickly."

Beck unexpectedly stepped in.

"Are you certain? This is a most urgent matter. Not a horse race."

"The end will come sooner than you think. Bertha's word."

Beck beamed profusely, then looked to Göring, who was more circumspect. The august minister, who was about to start a mass bloodletting, exhaled and leaned back.

"I fully expect you to be right, Bertha," the rotund minister said. "In the event you are not, then my personal response will come sooner than you think."

His paw reached across the table and this time patted my hand. Göring's hand was touching my wedding band – quite intentionally, I was sure. I was angry and might not have been able to keep it hidden. I straightened my posture and stared at him.

"You do not yet know the meaning of Bertha's word. But you will."

Göring guffawed at my audacity. He might have known the word "*chutzpah*". He then stood up and with Beck's help, donned his overcoat.

"Excellent, Bertha! You are a remarkable woman. And Beck, you were quite right. She is a most attractive Jew. So many are, so many are. It's a shame really!"

Beck was momentarily embarrassed but quickly fell back into official obsequiousness and feigned smile. It was he, not the august marshal, who slapped a hefty number of bills down on the table. They saw themselves out as I collected myself at the table. The money was twice the usual. It seems I was charging by the client's weight. A few moments after their car came to life and sped into the night.

Joshua came in from the bedroom and stood behind me, his hands comforting my shoulders with tender caresses. We looked at each other as two people might just after narrowly escaping death.

"We cannot do this much longer, Bertha."

THE MUNICH
TRAIN STATION

That was it. Joshua and I had danced with death and wanted no more of the Reich's bandleaders and dissonant music. We decided to flee to England by way of Holland. My parents finally agreed to leave as well. We packed all we could into two suitcases and looked about in sorrow at the belongings had to be left behind. It would fall into the hands of the landlord or a local Nazi official.

There was no train running from Munich to Amsterdam so we had to make a connection in Frankfurt. We would depart in the morning and reach Amsterdam in the late evening. The whole trip would take ten hours. From there we would board a ship to Portsmouth or any English port, whatever we could book passage on first. Our final destination was London. My father had colleagues at the London School of Economics who might be able to place him in the mathematics department. Another option was the New School in New York.

Though still August, the morning was cool as we hailed a cab and rode to the train station. The station was quite busy, all the more with the presence of soldiers, police, and uniformed Gestapo personnel. The latter force was the most fearsome as it was merging into the SS.

We walked quietly to the ticket booth and purchased our fares, paradoxically with the Reichsmarks Beck had given me the previous night. We boarded our train and waited. I calmed down as I sat and drifted into the sea of sensations. I saw trains and crowds and great suffering, I looked up and saw two SS officers standing above me. It was no dream.

"You are Frau Bertha Siegelman, are you not?" one of them asked.

I nodded.

"Come with us. The others too. Now!"

They escorted the four of us off the train as onlookers gawked briefly before turning away. We were packed into a car and taken back to our dwellings.

"You are to remain in your apartment and your parents will remain in their house. Those are my orders and you will kindly comply."

No Amsterdam, no London. We were stuck in Munich – and being watched.

Beck came by that night, unannounced of course. In fact, he didn't bother to knock. Joshua and I were startled as we sat on the parlor settee. A familiar face but hardly a comforting one, especially after that morning.

"We were disappointed in you two. Grievously disappointed – and after we made it clear to you how much we respected your work and how important it was to the nation. It has been decided from on high that you must remain right where you are, where we can ensure your continued service. It has been further decided that in order to punish you for this morning's disrespect, we shall place your parents in Buchenwald. It can be a rather unpleasant place, but then again it needn't be. Everyone gets what they deserve."

Rage built inside and was about to explode when Beck spoke coldly and firmly.

"Bertha my dear, you can go there as well, if you like. It's entirely up to you. To each his own. I tried to reason with Berlin on this but not everyone there is as understanding as am I."

I calmed myself and gauged the situation. I was not as helpless as Beck was suggesting. If he lost me, he'd lose guidance and he'd also lose a powerful benefactor.

"No harm is to come to my parents at your camp. Those are my terms. If they are unacceptable to you, then please explain that to your corpulent friend in Berlin, if you can."

He was angry but cornered.

"Your terms are of mutual benefit, Bertha my dear. Your parents will be taken care of. I shall see to it personally. As for you and your husband here, you can move about the city. You may shop for groceries and clothing. I suppose you will need candles as well. Oh, and you may visit the bank from time to time where you will see regular, generous deposits are made. You will be watched. That should be clear after this morning's little farce. Your business can proceed. Your customers can come and go. And I shall remain one of your most loyal clients. That will be all."

He bowed operatically and departed down the stairs, his footfalls making more noise than usual.

So, we had a deal. I would give guidance to Nazis and they would keep my family safe. I had Beck's word, one might say.

WAR COMES

On September 1, 1939 German troops invaded Poland. Shortly thereafter, country after country, including Britain and France, declared war on the Reich. Another world war had begun. The Jewish community in Munich was even more alarmed. The eruption of all-out war meant the rules were completely gone now. Berlin would not be limited to smashing windows and imprisoning a few thousand of us. What the army was doing to Poland, the Gestapo and SS would do to us. What good my deal with Beck would be, was uncertain.

There were more and more readings. Regular customers visited even more often and spread the word of my uncanny gift. Uncertainty and stress made the parlor all the busier. It had to be tidies up every night after the last client left. There were tailors, shop keepers, former doctors and lawyers, and retired people. I helped them keep hope. There were others.

Beck and Göring arranged to see me not long after Poland surrendered. The quick victory over Poland positively intoxicated them – and the rest of their gang in Berlin. That were giddy. I smelled brandy on them, especially when they laughed and boasted.

"You, my dear, were absolutely correct." Göring beamed. "It was easier than we thought. You should have seen all the prisoners and the look on their faces! I am impressed, deeply so. And you must be impressed by our might!"

"I am impressed by those who govern wisely."

"Ach, that," Göring replied with a wave of his small hand.

"We need to place your people where we can watch them. You can appreciate that. You above all."

"How are my parents?"

"All is well," Beck replied. "I have left instructions that their assignments are not too difficult and their rations are good. On that, you have my word."

I pondered the reliability of an SS officer's word for the briefest moment. Göring spoke up.

"We have more important things to be concerned with than the Jewish question. Everything in good time. The war in Poland is over but there are other countries that do not recognize the appropriateness of our actions and they are plotting against us as we speak. And that is where you come in, Bertha. Come, come. Let us sit and peer into the future once more."

We sat at the parlor table. I tried to calm myself but thoughts of my parents and the monstrosity of the men sitting across from me kept me on edge. I thought of the countryside, of birds and deer, of blue lakes and mountains. Nothing helped.

"I am sorry, gentlemen, but when I am not at ease I am unable to look into the sea of time. May I suggest you return tomorrow – or better, the next day."

"*You are not in a position to refuse us!*" the obsequious Beck shouted.

"I am by no means refusing you. I am merely saying that my gift will be more useful to you under different circumstances and without unannounced visits, though busy I know you both to be. And without implied threats, as with your outburst, Herr Beck."

Beck looked to Göring, who frowned for a moment, then nodded. They stood to leave. Beck tossed a pack of cigarettes on the table.

I sat alone in the salon until I was at ease. I walked into the sea and immersed myself.

Enormity all around me. Death and destruction, marching men and spreading fires, tanks and trains. I felt myself about to scream but fought it. I held my head in both hands and saw fire all around. All around me, all around the world.

Joshua came home. I returned from the sea and cried uncontrollably in his arms as I told him of my vision.

"What do you see, Bertha? Do you see anyone coming to our help?"

"No," I nodded. "Not in the near future at least. The war will go on and intensify and spread. It will be long. Many years."

"We have to get out of here. If we stay, we shall surely perish."

"But how? We are watched day and night."

"We could get rope and climb down to the alleyway. Then on to the rail station again or the Swiss border."

"They will kill our parents."

"Oh, Bertha! Don't you realize they'll kill them anyway? There are no laws or rules or norms or anything like common decency. Time is on their side, not ours. We can make a careful plan. We can hire a car or pay a truck driver to hide us in the back. What do you sense?"

"Oh, Joshua, I'm far too angst-ridden now. I only see flashes in a night sky."

"Then let's try to have a good night sleep and see tomorrow. We are not in immediate danger."

"Yes, my pact with them is in place for now."

Greta, a spirited elderly Lutheran woman who lived nearby, visited every few weeks. She knew our religious background and was ashamed by what was going on, at home and abroad. I had to apprise her that we were being watched and that anyone who came and went would be looked into. That angered her.

"I detest what this country has become! All this from that ridiculous band of lunatics who tried to take over Munich after a night of drinking in a bar. People today are afraid to speak their minds and they avoid old friends for fear of being branded unpatriotic. The fear is spreading. The Nazis have likeminded allies in foreign countries. The same gangsters but with different languages and uniforms. I will do what I see fit. What can those leather-jacketed hoodlums do to me? Kill me? I'm old and too cranky to do what they tell me to do."

"Greta, we love you. We respect you. But be careful. We have to be careful. So should you."

"I do what I damn well please!"

Courage was once defined as the golden mean between cowardice and foolhardiness.

In early 1940 Beck called to schedule a meeting. He might have surmised from his previous unannounced knock at my door with his stout marshal associate that I would be calmer and more helpful if an appointment were made. He might also have sensed that I detested and feared Göring more than I did him. It took no gift to discern that.

Beck was unexpectedly courteous.

"Ah, Bertha. We meet once again. It has been quite a while, has it not? Delightful to be in your dwelling once more. I hope our detail is keeping you safe. Such dangerous times we find ourselves in, such dangerous times."

My projection? So that's what they were for. We entered the salon and took our seats. The drapes had been drawn and the candles lit.

"I was impressed by your reading prior to the war in Poland. So was the Reichsmarschall and so were many others in Berlin. The names I must keep to myself for now. Well, Bertha, we have other scores to settle and they require similar uses of force. Yes, it is regrettable but there we have it."

"And you wish me to look into the matter."

"Exactly!"

"So we shall. But first, Herr Beck, I am most curious about one matter. Am I to understand that my readings figure in the Reich's decisions?"

"That is a rather difficult question, my dear."

Clearly it was. He fidgeted in the chair and looked about the room.

"I myself have thought about it and it is my considered opinion that your views are given consideration but many other things are important too. After all, Generals Keitel and Jodl and their large staffs write long analyses and give detailed presentations. However, my recommendation and your work of last summer has deeply impressed Berlin."

"Would it be fair to say that the generals are less impressed than the rest?"

"Oh my, yes. But enough of this we –"

"I could lie, you know."

Beck paused – long and hard.

"Indeed, you could. And indeed we would eventually know. There would be repercussions – at Buchenwald. Initially at Buchenwald."

"You know, Herr Beck, I could be mistaken. This is not an exact science as with mathematics. I have premonitions, feelings, sensations but they fall short of constituting equations."

"We have confidence in you, dearest Bertha. In the event of failure and disappointment it will be out of my power to offer any assistance whatsoever."

Oddly, and quite unexpectedly, I sensed sympathy for me and my situation.

"We have an understanding, Herr Beck. Now we have a reading to begin, interesting though this discussion has been."

I took his hands, closed my eyes, and drifted into the oceanic realm.

"More of the same….planes and trucks, tanks and men. Millions of them. Not the same direction as last time. Many flags, foreign ones. You will reach the sea."

"Reach the sea? Which sea?"

"The sea is cold and storm-ridden. And the end will come sooner than you think."

I opened my eyes and saw he was enthralled and a little frightened. It was a common enough look in my clients.

"Bertha's word."

His face brightened. There was softness inside this man, this man who could go weeks without showing any human qualities. Or was I misreading him? I didn't think so. He nodded almost in revery, then snapped into the role the Reich had assigned him and stood up.

"I have something in addition to your payment, my dear."

He placed a generous pile of Reichsmarks on the table and on top of it, an envelope. He bowed and left. I waited until his footfalls went away into the sounds of the street. My heart gladdened when I looked at the envelope. My name was on it, in my father's hand!

I tore it open.

> *My dearest child,*
>
> *Let your heart be at ease. I am in good health and feel no danger. I hope you are well and taking good care of your husband and yourself. You are our jewel, our love, our hope, and our future. I am sure that the uncertainty we are facing will soon end and we can be reunited. I cannot tell you how much I yearn for that day. It will come sooner than we think.*
>
> *With all my love,*
> *Father*

The letter lifted my spirits. But it was so brief. So painfully brief.

Not long thereafter, Germany invaded Denmark and Norway. This operation also proceeded well for the Reich. It was unlike telling someone they'd find a good job or meet an interesting person. I felt terrible. On the streets people were exuberant. They'd greet one another and go over the news and boast of a family member who'd taken part. The Reich to them was both wondrous and invincible. They loved war – as long as it brought swift victory. I felt that this war intoxication would lead to recklessness and greater danger. So did most in my community.

I was in a large, dank building with many long corridors and rooms. It was nighttime but the sun would shine brightly for a few moments before disappearing into the inky night. I walked down a corridor and heard my steps clacking off the bare brick walls like distant tanner blows. At the far end was father. I was delighted to see him but he was forlorn. He managed a faint smile and said, "Dearest Bertha, do not come closer. Please, stay away. Please, stay away." With that he turned and walked away down the corridor into darkness. A train whistle shrieked and I awoke in terror.

I lay in the dark and replayed what I saw over and over. There was no mistaking it. I would never see my father again.

MORE WARS

Intoxication would only bring more war. It was only a matter of time until Beck came calling once more. He called no more than two weeks after Norway fell to make an appointment. When we arrived at the table he presented a box of chocolates with a delicate bow.

"Stollwerck chocolates, *Schatzi*! I brought them from Cologne just for you, my special seer."

"You continue to surprise me, Herr Beck. I am grateful for the gift. My husband and I will enjoy them. Now, let us turn to business."

He was disappointed by my less than warm response.

"You were absolutely right again. Denmark and Norway gave us little trouble. Our men show great mastery of the art of war! So these chocolates are simply my small way of saying thank you and nothing more should be read into it."

He thanked me? Odd for an SS officer or anyone in a position of authority. I suppose I was helping his career as well.

"Herr Beck, I read of what is going on with the Jews. They are stripped of their property and put into decrepit parts of cities. Food is sparse, sanitation poor. What is the purpose? How does that serve your Reich?"

"Bertha, what I think doesn't matter. I am not the one in command. We have other things to look into this evening. Shall we?"

I didn't budge. My stare remained fixed. At length he sighed.

"I see what's going on and I admit it's not how I would order things. I would like to change things but I cannot. I try to help some people. You above all must realize that."

Well, to my surprise he had dispensed with officiousness and shown a small amount of regret and a larger quantity of concern for me.

"Let us sit in my parlor."

He sat and lit a candle with his lighter. He was ill at ease, unable to revert to form.

"Your harshness will lead to greater hostility toward Germany."

That angered him and a rebuke was building inside him.

"We are the most powerful military in the world! We have the finest leadership in the world! They know we will become more powerful through war and using undesirable people to make weaponry for our men."

"Hence Buchenwald."

"Yes."

"Hence the others."

"Just so. Now, as much as I enjoy exchanging private views with you – views I shall keep private, I might add – we have important work ahead of us. We have more plans for our neighbors. Perhaps you have heard talk of it while shopping or perhaps you know of it in your special way. To work, Bertha, to work! You know the purpose of our previous sessions. This one is no different."

He stared into the flame and waited. The pointed conversation annoyed me, yet understanding more of him and his bosses made the transition to the oceanic feeling easier.

There were the same legions of troops, rows of tanks, and skies darkened by planes. The direction was different but everyone knew that, especially the poor souls they'd soon attack.

"You will reach the sea once more...this time through dark woods...and you will do so without great cost at first. The end will come unexpectedly soon."

"And what of the enemy fortifications along the border?"

"I do not see them."

"Look harder, Bertha,"

"I still do not see them. Bertha's word."

"Hah! Excellent! Once again you have been invaluable. I must get back to Berlin at once! A deposit will be made in you bank tomorrow morning. Beck's word."

He dashed to the stairway and down to the street.

A few weeks later Germany defeated the French army and forced its British allies to evacuate from the beaches of Dunkirk. I take no pride in adding that the offensive struck through the Ardennes Forest and bypassed France's Maginot Line.

Joshua and I considered another escape attempt, but where and how? We were closely watched and dutiful guards were at every border checkpoint. They probably had our photos and knew the most of letting us slip by, Germany controlled lands to the east and north and if my senses were right, France was in for it soon. We knew a Swiss couple who would welcome us until the war ended, assuming it ever did. Greta was too old to get out but she told us of people who made it into Switzerland and encouraged us to do the same. She cautioned us in her witty way that border guards aren't as susceptible to bribes as they were in the good old days.

Joshua and I planned and debated and planned again. Finally we picked a date to make for Konstanz. That morning, however, I was filled with angst and knew I'd never get past even the slackest guard. A few weeks later we planned to travel to Friedrichshafen and hire or purchase a boat to take us across the lake to new lives. Again, my nerves got the better of me, and we stayed.

Beck called to arrange a session and told me he was bringing the man he brought before. He didn't want to mention a name on the telephone but I knew it would be Göring. I felt ill and had to calm myself. By this time France had fallen and the north was occupied by the Reich. Berlin was focusing on Britain now.

I opened the door and the two men dressed in pricey civilian attire with Nazi lapel pins strode right into the parlor and state themselves. In the case of one of them, rather noisily, with a grunt and sigh. Naturally, Göring was in the lead and he spoke first in a highly authoritative voice.

"You've done well so far but a new phase is underway and we need you to perform once more. France and the Low Countries are ours but some British soldiers were able to escape."

I was aware of that, though it was tens of thousands of them, not "some". Greta listened to BBC broadcasts and told us this was because Göring, master of the Luftwaffe. He had convinced Hitler his planes would annihilate the British before they could cross the Channel and reach safety on British soil. Göring failed – and was now seeking my counsel. That made for a sticky situation.

"The escape is in some respects an indication of Britain's resourcefulness when faced with defeat but it is of little importance in the long run. We are now devoting our energies to Britain. Air power will weaken them and a land invasion will end the war. All Europe will be ours. Tell me, Frau Siegelman, look into that realm you know so well and tell me how our effort will unfold?"

He sat back in his chair with a smug look, but one softened a measure of doubt in the back of his mind. Beck was clearly nervous. I closed my eyes and envisioned planes and water and cities as the ocean tides washed over me for several minutes. As much as I concentrated on Britain my senses kept turning to the east.

An enormous crimson blot spread across fields of ice and grain. And graves as far as anyone could see, all covered in oily red.

I shuddered with horror but saw opportunity. I opened my eyes and looked across the table. Göring was eager to hear my words, Beck remained uneasy. I realized he was worried about me.

"Britain is not Poland. Nor France, nor Holland. Britain will not bow before the Reich. It will continue the struggle for ever and ever."

Göring was taken aback and momentarily unnerved. I hid my joy at that moment.

"Bah!" Göring stood and paced angrily about the parlor.

Seeing his discomfort emboldened me and I elaborated. "Britain will have others in the struggle. It will not be a short affair. There are presently limits on how far I can see head. I cannot say that the victor will be you." I paused – quite deliberately and added a vague idea that came late to me. "Someone will fly to Britain."

This time my joy was discernible, I'm sure. Göring was caught off guard. He glared at me for painfully moments, then leaned over the table and spoke with clenched teeth.

"And let us be clear, gypsy woman. Just who should fly to Britain? Are you even suggesting that I should take off from Tempelhof and head to an airfield near London?"

"Not you, Herr Reichsmarschall. One of you. Someone high up. And not 'should'. I said 'will'. One of you *will* fly to Britain."

"To bomb them into submission! That is the only reason."

Without any control, images in my mind turned into words and I murmured them over and over.

"Flight, fall, talk...flight, fall, talk...."

"What nonsense! You are babbling! Beck, this gypsy is babbling."

Göring rushed around the table clumsily and slapped me. I fell to the hard wooden floor and came out of my sea. He stepped back and Beck helped me to my chair and daubed his handkerchief on my bloodied lip.

"She may be wrong this time, Herr Reichsmarschall. I'm sure she is. Let us not forget. However, that she has been helpful in the past and she will be helpful in the future."

Göring's wrath shifted from me to Beck. An underling had helped a Jew.

"This woman has not told me what she saw in that realm of hers! She has told me what a Jew wants to see! The Fatherland embattled! The Reich under attack! Flight! Never! And you, Beck, if I want your views, I'll summon you to Berlin and ask for them!"

"Flight, fall, talk...flight, fall, talk...." I continued to murmur through swollen lips.

Göring stormed out the door and marched noisily down the stairs to his car.

Beck remained with me and tended to my injury. Appearances and sensations suggested genuine concern – hardly anything I expected from an SS officer, hardly anything I wanted from one. I was puzzled but perhaps a bit touched.

"Why, Herr Beck? Why do you show such consideration for a Jew – and in front of that oaf?"

He became sad and looked at me for long moments. He placed a pile of Reichsmarks on the table, bowed slightly, and left for Göring's waiting car. A door slammed and the car drove off. I was convinced that my reading made me emerge on top, though of course Göring didn't know it yet.

ANOTHER TRY,
A COSTLY FAILURE

J oshua and I decided to attempt another escape. The reading and
dream were simply too frightening. If they overstated reality a
hundred-fold we were still in for hell. We had observed that the
guard detail was less alert on early Sunday mornings, possibly because
of revelry the night before, so we selected the following Sunday as the
best time. No premonitions, purely logical calculations. We packed
small bags and gathered our money and a few pieces of jewelry.

Saturday night we tied sheets together for a makeshift rope and
climbed down to the alley. Joshua had read of that technique in
a crime mystery in his youth. From there we found a drowsing
cabdriver and requested a lift to Memmingen, about a hundred
kilometers west. He looked at us with suspicion but a copious number
of Reichsmarks eased his concerns and soon we were racing down
the Autobahn until we reached the Memmingen bus terminal. From
there we would head for Friedrichshafen or Konstanz, whichever we
could head for first.

The terminal was packed with soldiers and security forces. So
young, so confident, so eager to play their part in the great play that
I knew would be a ghastly tragedy. When their bus was announced
they stood tall, hugged family members, and boarded their buses for
what could only suspect was the east. I felt sorry for them. There were
so many naive people caught up in the National Socialist delusion
that was made all the more appealing by those quick victories.

Joshua noticed I was deep in thought.

"What lies ahead for us, dear? Is that where your mind was just now?"

"I'm too anxious for the ocean, Joshua. How many of these boys will never see Germany again? It isn't an answerable question, I know."

A young private hugged his parents and saluted before heading for his journey.

An hour later a bus came to a halt and the speaker announced a departure for Friedrichshafen. That was us. We stood and walked calmly to the idling vehicle, showed our tickets, and boarded. In a few minutes we were on our way south. There was little traffic and we arrived in mid-afternoon. As we disembarked, I saw two men on the platform looking at us. One nudged the other and they headed straight for us. There was no mistaking who they were. There was no mistaking who we were. The took us by the arms, compared our faces to photographs, and whisked us away.

We were driven back to Munich and hastened into our apartment, a guard at the door. The next morning we were awakened by the sounds of boots in the salon.

"Bertha! Joshua! Get out here now, the both of you!"

It was Beck, of course.

"Sit down! Foolish! Foolish! Foolish! You are well taken care of here and I see that your parents have it good. Nonetheless, you betray my trust and try to leave Germany when it needs you most. I am not your worst problem, believe me. There are men above me who are less restrained than I am and they want to mete out punishments to your families. I have asked them to let me deal with you my way. For this you should be grateful."

He paused but we dared not speak. I felt like an unruly student at Prussian cadet school in the days of the Kaisers.

"You are under house arrest. You are not to leave without escort. Not from the front door and not by climbing down bedsheets as in a tawdry *Krimi*. The guards will bring you food and other necessities.

No visitors, no clients. The Reich will take care of your expenses. and I will see that it does so rather generously. Consider this your last warning!"

Beck came back a few days later in a different mood. He was somber and reluctant to speak, as though he cared about our feelings, or probably just mine. I was intrigued by his demeanor but dreaded what was to come. Anyone would.

"Frau Siegelman, it is with a heavy heart that I bring sad news this day. You father was killed in Buchenwald yesterday."

"Killed?"

"Executed, it seems. The order came from high up, I assure you."

"Oh my god, he's gone? My father's gone?"

A dozen images of his death flashed before, each one contradicting the other. I fell into Joshua's arms and wept for several minutes.

"What of my mother? What have you done with her?"

"I have no information about her at present but she has not shared the fate of your father. But the message should be clear. Any more nonsensical dashes for Switzerland will end just as the first two did. Do not take the SS and Gestapo for fools and do not take my superiors to be fair-minded. Inattentiveness to your duty will bring only more suffering – and more deaths." He signaled his departure with a bow and parting words. "I am sorry for your loss. It must be painful but we all have losses during such times."

"My *loss*? You killed him!"

"It was not on my order. It came from far higher than the Sturmbannführer level I occupy for now. "I am sorry... truly sorry. I wish...oh, it doesn't matter what we wish."

He was out of his element as an officer and functionary of death. He stated in silence, perhaps awaiting my gratitude, then left as somberly as he came in.

I became deeply depressed and listless – and useless for my calling. My father was gone and my mother's fate uncertain. Joshua and I were in the same precarious position. I spent hours looking out to the skyline in melancholic reflection, recalling my childhood with both parents and imagining how father met his end. He did so bravely, I was sure. I could only hope it was quick. Scenes stabbed me at night and I dared not peer into the sea of past events for certainty. He was gone and in time I realized I had to persevere – and get back at the bastards however I could.

UNDERSTANDING THEM

Greta was difficult to deal with. Her family knew that, so did her neighbors. When the security detail blocked her from entering my building she put up a fight. Words flew. Her fists came down on Gestapo shoulders. The guards were amused but they had their orders. An officer who was patrolling the block came by and told the men to let the poor old lady up for an hour.

"Thanks heavens there is a man with some intelligence left in this country! And what is your name young man."

"I'm Gruppenführer Lauman, madam. These men do as I instruct them. You may have one hour upstairs."

She smiled graciously at him, then glared reproachfully at the guards.

Seeing her again was invigorating. Her verve and gestures were a most welcome break from the sameness of our dwelling.

"I know what's afoot in this country and all around it." She leaned toward us with a mischievous smile and whispered, "I listen to the BBC at night! If they catch me I'll tell them I was listening to Lord Haw." Joshua and I were quizzical. "He's a British fool who gives propaganda broadcasts from Berlin."

A noose flashed before my eyes.

"Britain has won for now. Göring's mighty Luftwaffe is not faring well. In fact the Royal Air Force is sweeping them from the skies! He is not present at as many official ceremonies in Berlin anymore."

"Will they shoot him?"

"No, he's too big to shoot, literally and figuratively! He just isn't as powerful as he once was."

"Will there be peace?" Joshua asked.

"I don't think so. Oh! Did you hear about Hess? Rudolph Hess, that is."

"I only know the name as one of Hitler's confidantes," he said.

"Not anymore!" Greta exclaimed before lowering her voice. The fool flew to Britain and parachuted to the ground in order to begin peace negotiations! A mystic told him to do it."

"It was not me, Greta! I assure you it was not me. Still, I did say something like that to a client a few months ago, albeit rather vaguely and metaphorically."

"I never ask of your clients, Bertha. You know that. Perhaps word reached Hess somehow. In any event, the British locked him up, probably in a lunatic asylum."

"So the war will continue," Joshua murmured.

"It will, it will. I think that even though Hitler signed a pact with Stalin just before they devoured Poland, Hitler mistrusts him. He might even fear him."

"They are in agreement about taking over small countries," said Joshua.

"For now," Greta replied quickly. "When they run out of small countries, they will come to blows. And that could well be the ruin of Hitler and his Reich."

"As it was for Napoleon and his empire," I said.

"However, many millions will die first," Joshua said. "I don't understand the Nazis attraction to mysticism. Look at the buildings and roads and art – modern in every respect. Look at the engineering and medical advancements – all based on science."

Greta listened closely and began a response.

"True enough, but there's another dimension to those men. They have immersed themselves in ancient myths of Germanic warriors, racial superiority, and glory in war and conquest. Hermann battling the Romans in a deep forest. Siegfried battling all comers to win the ring of the Nibelungen. And amid an immense war that has much of the world against them, the big shots are eager to consult with mystics."

"Aha!" Joshua exclaimed. "Hermann sought augurs before he clashed with the legions deep. Hannibal did the same before he crossed the Alps. Frederick needed to consult seers as three armies closed in on him. The Nazis are ignorant of history and the military sciences. They mistrust those who are knowledgeable of such things. And they have so much more territory to conquer."

"I held a reading with one high-ranking Nazi. His name shall remain undisclosed for now. But during my reading I saw him flying in the last war and returning to his squadron. At night he anguished over why he had lived and so many others had died, even though they were more experienced and more talented than he. He came to believe in destiny. There are unknown forces determining the fates of men – and of Germany. I wonder if Hitler had similar thoughts in the trenches. I can't say but both men know that Germany lost the previous war and must use every resource to see it does not lose this one."

"You two should write the unseen history of the Third Reich one day," Greta said with a wan smile. "I can tell you that in my travels to the countryside I came across many people – whole villages – that celebrated the rise of the Nazis. Their lives were steeped in the blood of farm animals and the soil that gave them all sustenance. The precarious nature of their lives make them look for signs of good favor and for heroic figures promising a return to a mighty nation."

"It will be a long night," Joshua sighed.

A knock came and everyone froze.

"You hour is up," came the gruff voice.

I looked out on the street and saw Greta look up and wave to me, then say a few choice words to the guard detail. I hope she gave them hell.

Joshua and I were prisoners – well fed and well housed but prisoners all the same. Food and rent were paid for, the latter brought to the door by what I called Beck's domestic workers. If we needed candles or new drapes, they were brought at once.

We began to read the Bible and pray before meals. I asked Joshua if the guards would bring us a menorah but never pushed our luck.

Joshua came up with the idea of exercising. Every afternoon, an hour before dinner, we walked in place and did stretches. Joshua knew them from his gymnasium days when he played football. I drew the line at what were called "pushups".

After dinner we looked out onto the streets. There were no blackouts yet so the view was pleasant and often delightful. Civilians and more and more soldiers walked by. The latter strode about in small groups, often marching in step, singing ribald songs, and laughing heartily. I felt sorrow for them – and saw trains filled with people heading east. It was the autumn of 1940.

THE FÜHRER SITS
AT MY TABLE

B eck called and said he would arrive in an hour. He was stern and very nervous. I heard the guards come to attention and soon enough I heard Beck's boots on the stairs.

"Greetings, Herr and Frau Siegelman. Forgive me for putting aside the pleasantries that normally begin our meetings but there's an urgent matter. In the past I have entrusted you with the presence of a revered member of our government and today I am doing the same with an even more revered figure."

"I doubt it will be Rudolf Hess," I said.

Beck did not immediately catch the sarcasm.

"Frau Siegelman! There will be no more of your witticisms! The Führer will meet with Benito Mussolini here in Munich next week and he has instructed me to arrange a meeting."

"A meeting with whom?"

"With you, of course. My presence should tell you that. The Führer will be here in one week."

"Here? The Führer is coming here to seek her guidance?" Joshua exclaimed.

"Exactly. We are all aware that if Bertha doesn't feel comfortable her gift is not as discerning. So, I suggest you rest, prepare yourself as you see fit, and be in top form."

We all have moments when we are unsure if we are awake or

deep in slumber. For me this was one of those moments but alas I was wide awake.

"I cannot abide his presence! I'll spew out my hatred for him and all he stands for! I'll demand he account for my father!"

"That would be unwise – and for reasons not unrelated to your father's demise." Beck spoke more gently than before. "Remember I am far more reasonable than those of above me. It is not a matter for discussion. You will meet with the Führer – here – and you will be in top form. Please collect yourself. You have one week."

He was on his back foot, defensive, vulnerable.

"Reinhard...Reinhard, you are not one of them, at least not entirely."

"Ah well, we all have roles to play in life. I was a believer in the first act. Germany was proud and strong again – and there is nothing wrong with feeling pride in your nation."

"And the second act?"

"Pride can become arrogance and heavy-handedness. Parades can become invasions – too easily. And Buchenwald. I saw it as a place where enemies were put for the common good. Now...it is a place to break people, crush them – and yes, kill them."

"Like my father."

"Regrettably so. I learned of it only after the event. He was shot to death. It was quick and there is mercy in that."

"Where are his remains?"

"Burned. Burned along with others."

I saw flashing images of a mass grave and long trains.

"What of the final act?" Joshua asked softly.

Beck stiffened and reverted to his role.

"I do not know the final act. No one does. Not even your wife. Now, the Führer will be here in one week. Do not disappoint him. Good evening, Herr and Frau Siegelman."

He bowed and left.

"How will you deal with this visitor, Bertha my dear?"

"I cannot be sure at all. I am sure of one thing, however. I am glad we did not get that menorah."

"Oh, Bertha!"

My sense of humor was intact. Of that there was no doubt. I
had to steel myself for what was coming. We exercised more often
and more extensively, as though we were preparing to meet Max
Schmeling in the ring. The regimen imposed discipline, vigor, and
confidence.

The week was soon up. I awaited Beck's telephone call. It came
in the late afternoon and a guard was sent up to take Joshua away
from the apartment and ensure I had no weapons. Beck told me the
guard would take him to a fine restaurant. I found that somewhat
reassuring but his being taken away was surely an implicit threat.

I looked out the window to rainy skies and saw a large Mercedes
approach with two escort vehicles ahead of it. I half expected to see
Nazi flags fluttering from the Mercedes's front fenders but that was
the stuff of newsreels and rallies. This was a clandestine meeting
with a psychic. A guard opened the door and opened an umbrella
for a man I could not yet see.

Up the stairs they came. I breathed deeply and opened the door.
There were four of them, Beck, two other SS officers, and a man
of average height with his trademark Oliver Hardy mustache. One
officer took off Hitler's coat, revealing a doubled-breasted suit with
a swastika armband but none of the Iron Crosses and other military
devices I had seen in photographs.

Beck began introductions but Hitler waved a dismissive hand.
I saw an altogether ordinary man. Suit aside, there was nothing
obviously remarkable about him. There was no commanding presence
or charisma. He seemed no different than someone I might pass on
the street or see at a newsstand. So this was the Führer. His aura
came chiefly from searchlights and blustery speeches and above all,
adoring, cheering crowds. He struck me as an Austrian corporal with
an eye for the show – and a desperate audience. If I may say without
sounding elitist, Adolf Hitler had a decidedly low-class look to him.

Beck glared at me and I bowed slightly. Beck showed more of a reaction than his boss. I wondered if Hitler expected me to exchange pleasantries in a fawning manner but happily he walked toward the parlor. sat at the table, and cleared his throat.

"I am told – and by reliable people, at least for the most part – that you are able to look into the future and see events. I knew such people in Vienna and came to trust one or two of them. The rest were carnival frauds. But you. You have a remarkable talent that can be of use to me."

"It is true...at times," I said softly. Looking into his eyes more stably than I thought I could. His eyes darted about the room, nervously. He cleared his throat.

"Your record is quite good and we shall see how good it is this evening."

We sat across from each other, curtains drawn, candles lit. A feared his coldness could extinguish the flickering flames. I sensed much of him at the doorway, much more as he sat near me. Resentments from boyhood, fear in the war; compassion for others vanished early if it was ever there at all. Thirst for vengeance, hatred of so many and no trust my people. He knew I was Jewish but kept that information hidden from most of his mind.

"You sense so much, dear woman. You drink it all in. Do not let any of it fall from your lips."

He knew things. Things others don't. That worried me. Nonetheless, I was able to drift into my ocean.

"I have a meeting here in Munich, perhaps you have read about. Or perhaps not. Mussolini of Italy and his generals will hold talks with me and my generals."

Sensation after sensation came. Moments passed. Hitler stood and looked around the room, then stared out the window, before returning to stand over a candle on the table. Its light flickered over his dark hair and insecure eyes. He wanted more war, perhaps more than those around him.

"Mussolini, wants more."

"So do we all. What does Il Duce want more of?"

"More power...as much as he can grab. He wants to lead his

legions like the Caesars of ancient times. He wants to conquer and boast."

"Interesting. Most interesting."

He leaned down between the flames and me, searching my eyes. I momentarily felt fear but it passed sooner than I could have imagined. He had little regard for me as a human. That capacity left him while in the trenches. He knew I had a power and for brief moments he saw me as a medieval sorceress. His question at that moment was could he trust me to tell the truth.

"Go on."

"Il Duce wants as much glory and power as you now have…and he wants to hold sway over you and be your master. Germania will make Rome more glorious than Berlin."

"And what shall I do?"

"You are wary of him…Rome shall never overshadow Berlin. You are your own master and that of all Europe."

"Did you hear that, gentlemen?" he asked of his fawning aides. "She knows me well and knows how I think and act! She knows of my unalterable will! Extraordinary!"

His eyes sparkled for once and her looked about to Beck and the other two. Their smiles came swiftly and dutifully. He stood and paced about, then returned to the cradle on the table.

"There is much riding here, woman. More than you can know. Is there anything else you would like to add."

"Only this."

I paused and for a few moments this deranged man was my prisoner. Beck looked at me pleadingly. I stared into Hitler's cold eyes and matched his intensity.

"Mussolini may want to saddle you but he does not know of your unalterable will. His blunders must not be yours."

"Yes, yes. He is a buffoon and I am not. I have a destiny, he does not. Anything else?"

"Only this – Bertha's word."

"Bertha's word! Just as you said, Beck! Just as you said!"

He clasped his hands and smiled triumphantly before signaling his watch dogs that the reading was over. The four of them headed for the door. Beck turned to me and sent a glance of gratitude.

Joshua was brought home shortly later in good spirits."

"How was your dinner? I hope you didn't partake of pork, dear."

"I had roast beef but I appreciate your concern with dietary laws while you met Hitler. How did it go?"

"Better than I could hope. I read him well, saw what was coming, at least some of it."

"Did you win his confidence?"

"Oh yes. Undoubtedly. I expect a return visit."

"Can you use him?"

"I believe so."

"And you will try to bring him down."

"Bertha's word."

THE CLIENT RETURNS

Very few people telephoned us anymore. Most people knew of the Gestapo detail outside the building and assumed the line was tapped. We assumed the same thing. When the phone rang it was likely to be Beck or one of his colleagues in the death's head corps who wanted answers. One autumn morning I expected Beck to telephone and was miffed when he did not. Joshua and I enjoyed tea and a broadcast of Wilhelm Furtwängler and the Berlin Philharmonic.

"Do you recall the word Furtwängler used to describe Germany a few years ago, Bertha?"

"I believe the word was 'swinishness' and it was well-chosen.

"That's it. Yet he kept his position."

"Yet he kept his neck."

Boots in the stairwell, the door swung open, and then Hitler and two subordinates stormed in. No Beck that day. We stood slowly, unsure of what was coming or if we were going.

"Ah, you are eating. You were absolutely right about Mussolini. He'll not get the better of me."

He was elated, like a man who'd just been married. Joshua and I were stunned, though as far as Hitler was concerned, Joshua was furniture or invisible. I must confess the thought of offering this ebullient madman some tea, albeit brewed from nuts, crossed my mind.

"And you were right about the British too. Yes, yes, Göring told me all about that. We will continue to hammer them though. It's welcome that you give us good news and bad news too. It shows you have clairvoyance and honesty and that prepares me for what is coming. Most seers were complete charlatans! They only tell people what they want to hear. In my position I need facts, the truth. I have all the flattery I need."

"And so you've come to me."

He sat at the parlor table and Joshua took his leave. Hitler's ebullience abruptly ended and he looked broodingly at nothing in particular. He was sinisterly determined.

"What can we expect from those people across the Channel? They have resilience. I'll give them that. What is coming. I need to be prepared."

I relaxed, breathed deeply, and looked into the sea. It was difficult. Beck wasn't there and the break with custom concerned me. Had he disappointed this man in front of me? Not important now, I told myself. At length I received impressions.

"The British have great power. They will not defeat the Reich. We all know that. But neither will the Reich defeat them. They pose no threat for the time being. They will seek support from overseas."

"That was expected. But who will win?"

"I cannot see a victor in this war with Britain. My powers cannot look out into infinity."

"Bah! You need to look harder! Concentrate! Concentrate!"

I closed my eyes and did my best but the result was the same.

"I am sorry. I cannot see that far into the future. The glimmers are not coalescing into a discernible image."

His forehead knitted. He was angry but in time it was clear I was not the object of his ire.

"There is something now."

His wrath dissipated and he became intrigued and hopeful. I felt in control again. I also felt gleeful. even mischievous. I chose my words carefully and imparted them sternly.

"Your actions are pissing off a major power. They are of the same race. It will not remain at arm's length for long. It will come to Britain's aid."

"America! I know that is coming. President Rosenfeld is controlled by Jews and he will come after us eventually. We have surprises in store for them though. That I can tell you."

"I do not see this major power in the west."

He was bewildered and took a deep breath to prepare.

"Astonishing what you sense. It was only a thought in my mind. I never mentioned it to that incompetent Göring."

My sense was that he was ambitious. No, it was far more than that. This nervous Austrian wanted immense power – more than anyone ever had. That yearning radiated from him and filled the room. It was twinned with a dilettantish mistrust of experts – economists, historians, and generals. He felt destined to succeed where Caesar and Charlemagne, Frederick the Great and Napoleon, had failed.

My senses were alloyed with Greta's conviction that once Hitler and Stalin defeated small countries, they would come to blows. I would later learn that Hitler was attracted to Russia's vastness and wanted its open steppes to be colonized by hearty Germany farmers.

Hitler's will for power, mistrust of others, and solidifying confidence in me filled me with an ambition of my own. I didn't want land or high office. I wanted to do as much for the world as a young woman could.

"I need to know more – now!"

He raised a fist and was about to slam it onto the table but held back.

"I need only a few more minutes." I said quietly as I concentrated deeper into my thoughts. The room obligingly fell silent. You have never experienced eeriness like that in the room just then. Indeed, I was concentrating, but not in the realm of the ocean. I was using my gifts for history and politics to chart a path and point him down it.

"Victory is in store…to the east. Immense battlefields, mass graves stretch to the horizon and beyond. Yes, victory and enduring glory and power for the man who leads the way."

"And your counsel this day?" His words were soft, almost prayerful.

"March to the east, with all your might, all your aspirations, all your will. Show no concern for allies or naysayers. They only wish to thwart you."

I stared into his eyes with all the intensity I could summon. He was taken, transfixed, on my hook. A smile formed beneath that little mustache. It wasn't the smile you'd see in official photographs or newsreels. It was genuine and it looked out of place and surreal.

"It is most welcome to have the acquaintance of one so talented, one who has vision and courage and will. Each of us has an extraordinary yet different form of vision and together, well, together there is nothing we cannot accomplish."

I continued to stare into him in silence, pondering what events were being set into motion. He sensed disapproval.

"You do not have to think of us as partners. In fact, I do not think we are even on the same side on every matter. Above all, Frau Bertha, do not for one moment think we each need the other. I fully expect future meetings to be as productive as this one. Fully!"

I remained at the table as the men left. I had placed him on a path of destruction. It would cost many lives but any path he took would do that. My counsel set him on a path that would lead to his ruin and my vengeance.

Joshua did not feel comfortable with the ruse. He was sure it would lead to our deaths. I pointed out that we were involved in a war that was about to become bigger, probably bigger than the bloodletting of 1914-1918. I had a part to play. I wasn't going to lead a charge or drop a bomb but I had a mission. We had heard Churchill's speech about fighting on the beaches, fields, and streets. Berlin had broadcast it. His words brought inspiration. I wanted mine to bring destruction, even if it meant my own as well.

Joshua kissed me as a way of consenting.

"I want you to live through the destruction, Bertha. I want you to go on no matter what."

I looked at him as I pondered the implication, then gave him my consent.

The meeting earlier that day replayed in my mind incessantly, even in sleep. Reading and dream merged into a vivid panorama that would frighten Goya or Dürer or Bosch.

Crimson red, unspeakable agonies, mass graves, billows of smoke, and endless trains. Dreadful images from books of wars past came to me – trenches, barbed wire, corpse-strewn fields, fire, and gas – but they were less horrifying than what I saw at night.

I woke up several times to the comfort of Joshua's loving arms.

I heard a commotion outside our building and scurried for the window, fearful that it was Beck or his rotund associate or the one with the circus-clown mustache. An elderly woman was telling the guard detail off and brandishing an umbrella. I opened the window to better appreciate the scene.

"I am a German citizen and I am entitled to visit my neighbor!"

"Hello, Greta!"

"Do you know this crone?" a guard called up to me as he prepared to receive a spirited blow from an umbrella.

"Indeed I do. And so does your detail commander – Gruppenführer Lauman. He has authorized her to visit for one hour."

I omitted the small matter of the authorization having been given weeks ago and for one day only, but they made no investigation and Greta was on her way up.

"These petty little thugs in uniform are a plague upon Germany."

"They may be thugs but they can be violent and cruel," Joshua chided.

"Nein, nein! They wouldn't dare harm an old woman."

"Oh but they would. Come, let us sit down. We sent out for a bottle of wine and the guards brought a decent one this time. A French one," Joshua was pleased to announce.

"So, grapes are among the fruits of victory in the west."

"I shall get the glasses now. Let us sit. I regret to say that our spacious wine cellar is closed for the duration of the war!"

The wine was poured and the conversation flowed. It probably worked better under those conditions. We discussed ongoing roundups of dissidents and undesirables, the international situation, and my readings with high-ranking but unnamed figures. I added my concern that the war would be long and nightmarish.

"You two are young. You should try to flee again."

"Ach, Greta. We are watched night and day. Our last attempt failed and in retaliation the SS killed my father."

"Oh, my heavens! Where?"

"Buchenwald."

"I hear of people being sent there all the time. I do not hear of them returning. I overheard two solders say the prisoners are beaten and starved."

"Remember that those guards downstairs are cut from the same cloth as their friends at Buchenwald. If we make another break for it they will shoot my mother, wherever she is, and Joshua's parents as well."

"Their pitiless nature is just my point. Your people are all in great danger, no matter what they do. In Poland a dark process is already underway. It's all the more reason you should make another attempt. I can help."

"We do not want to involve you, Greta!"

"Listen, my late husband built this block of apartments and I will tell you there is a tunnel connecting the basements of your building and mine. It was designed to haul away coal ashes from the furnaces but they have fallen into disuse. You can make your way to my building, then out the alley."

"Oh, Greta! No! Even if we made it out of Germany, those hoodlums downstairs would come for you," Joshua said.

"That Lauman downstairs would be at your door in short order," I added. "The train and bus stations are closely watched. The guards have our photographs. They've probably committed our images to memory."

"There are areas of open farmland along the border. Yes, there is barbed wire but there are gaps used by smugglers. A farmer I know can show you the gaps. And the patrols? They are old men. Many were crippled in the last war. Getting around them would present no challenge for two young healthy people."

Greta's looked like a mischievous child.

A knock sounded on the door.

"Your hour, which I did not authorize, is up!" Lauman barked.

"Shut up!" Greta snapped instantly.

We whispered to Greta that we would keep her plan in mind. She picked up her umbrella and opened the door abruptly, unnerving Lauman.

"I am coming, you revolting young man! No respect for old people these days! None!"

ANOTHER ATTEMPT

Every few weeks Beck came by for a reading. He was stationed in Berlin but his intelligence work brought him to Vienna, Stuttgart, and Munich. More often than not he brought fellow officers, majors, colonels and an occasional general. They sought insights on careers and romantic interests rather than on geopolitics and grand strategy. They were true believers. Their faith in the Führer and had no doubt that the Reich would be ever victorious.

It was troubling and consoling at the same time to see that men who wore the death's head and lightning runes had romantic interests. Some even had children in school. Nonetheless, if ordered, they would shoot me without hesitation. Maybe one of them had shot my father. I looked upon work with them as practice in reaching the ocean and judging the hopes and expectations.

Their payments were prompt and generous. We had plenty of money but consumer goods were becoming scarce. That is what the guards told me. They had become our errand boys. Wine, potatoes, tablecloths – anything really – would be ours in a matter of hours. We continued to joke about ordering a menorah, especially late in the year.

Beck was a welcome departure from the true believers. We conversed about day-to-day things and readings with him revealed surprising depth and tragedy. A somber look often came across his countenance which I took as a sign he was unhappy with the Reich and uneasy about the Russian campaign. I also took it as regret that he had not stopped my father's execution.

In one reading I determined that he was deeply saddened about father's death. More than once he asked if there was anything else we needed and if the guards were quiet and respectful. I asked about my mother and Joshua's parents and he replied that he did not know. I was sure he did, however.

My readings of SS men and concern that Hitler would indeed invade Russia in coming months worried us profoundly. My dreams of horror in the east came every few nights with lengthening durations and stronger intensities. The worst of them caused me to awaken my husband to help calm me. We felt we knew more of what was to come than anyone in Berlin or Moscow, including the evil men on top. Jews and others were being rounded up. More camps were being built. Dark rumors came out of Poland.

The torment was worsened by confinement. Had we been able to walk in parks or drive into forests we might have come back refreshed and tranquil. But we became what Americans call "stir crazy."

Anxieties spread, clear thinking diminished. We decided to talk to Greta about her plan. It was late 1940.

Greta came by for her hour-long visit and we told her of our decision. We snuck down into the cellar and she pointed to a part of the brick wall just above the cold floor that would lead to the cellar of her building. She'd already made the measurements. We had a hammer and chisel to gradually chip away at the cement and bricks. It would be a laborious process as it had to be done slowly and quietly. She would do the same, as best she could, from her side of the wall.

We set to work the next day. Joshua scraped and chiseled while I stayed upstairs watching the guards. Traffic offered a welcome din. A noisy tram gave the chance to deliver a few hard blows. The first few bricks were the toughest. Once they were gone, the others gave way more easily. By evening of the third day there was enough room for us to crawl and shimmy our way into Greta's cellar. Now we had to wait for her to arrange for her collaborator to pick us up and drive us to a farm near the Swiss border.

Greta came by a few days later. We thought it would signal the guards that we were settled into a routine.

"I read of our generals meeting with counterparts in Hungary and Romania. They are not there to sign trade deals and increase cultural ties. I do not have your gift, dear Bertha, but I sense bad things are coming in that part of Europe."

A flash of fear raced through me. Something was amiss.

"My farmer friend will be here on Monday. He drives into Munich on that day every few weeks to buy a few things and see his sister. He will drive into the alley early Tuesday morning at the melodramatic hour of dawn, take on two passengers, and drive back home. He lives ten kilometers from a forlorn part of the border and has snuck through the wire into Switzerland a couple times a year."

I saw barbed wire stretching to the horizon, but not in the countryside.

"You place great confidence in him, eh," said Joshua.

"Indeed, I do. He and his family did business with my father. His brother and my brother served in the same regiment at Ypres in 1914!"

"We can compensate him most handsomely," I said.

"That won't be necessary, but I doubt he would refuse."

The next few days passed excruciatingly slowly and a sense of dread fell over me. Joshua asked if we should call the whole thing off but I stuck to the plan, albeit warily.

Beck came by, more to check in on us than to solicit my professional views. His stay was short and Joshua and I settled in the parlor listening to the Berlin Philharmonic performing Beethoven's Violin Concerto. It was a favorite, especially the second movement with its heartrending solo passages. Erich Röhn was playing masterfully.

I felt more dread as I sensed Beck was tied to dark operations. I saw the bricks in the cellar keeping people in, not leading us out. Dread became nausea and vertigo. Joshua held me and encouraged me to drink a little wine. Nothing helped. The room was spinning, rushing sounds whirled around me. The door was kicked in and Lauman and two guards barged in. They had Greta.

The welts and blood on her face caused me to throw up violently. The guards hurled her to the floor. She kneeled and hurled insults.

"You disgusting goons! You can beat me but you will never break me! If I were a few years younger it would be you two bleeding on the ground!"

"You did not think we would find that gap in the cellar wall," Lauman said matter of factly. "That is unfortunate."

"Your day is coming. There are too many good Germans," Greta spat.

"Not as many as you think, old fool! It was your farmer friend who told us." Greta's spirit gave way suddenly. "He knows Jews for what they are – enemies! Thank God there are patriots like him and always will be!"

"He is a coward, not a patriot," she said in sorrow. I am ashamed to be German. I am ashamed of what this country has become."

Lauman drew his Luger, chambered a round, and shot her in the head. Though she was lifeless, he put another round into her temple. I screamed as blood spurted and flowed across the floor. Joshua grabbed hold of me.

Lauman aimed his pistol at me and paused a few agonizing seconds.

"No. Would that I could. But my orders are clear. Ah, but my orders say nothing about this man – this Siegelman Jew."

He aimed at Joshua's forehead, then paused. I cannot say why. Perhaps he thought his orders had not explicitly authorized killing him or he feared that my husband's death would make me less useful. That of course would have angered his superiors greatly and he might have a dozen firearms aimed his way. He re-holstered the pistol.

"Get the traitor's body out of here!" His anger gave way to sarcasm. "And you two, clean this place up immediately. It is a disgrace."

He would have entombed her in the cellar wall if there had been room.

Beck arrived the next day, His expression was grim, as expected.

"I do not understand you two. How is it that I am not able to make it clear that your cooperation comes along with privileges – ones that I assure you people like you do not have in many other places. The camp system is growing with every passing week. There are more barracks, more work to be done, more punishments to administer, and more trains."

"Where is my mother? Where are my husband's parents?" My words were deliberate and pointed.

"That is not for you to know, especially after your recent foolishness. You must act as though you may never see them again. And if there is any more such foolishness, you may never see each other again."

Cold swept over Joshua and me. I felt numb.

Images of our parents came before me followed by flashes from a dozen rifles.

ADVANCES

December of 1940 was both cold and lonely. We no longer had any visitors, at least not ones we welcomed. The number of guards had increased and they went about their rounds with more determination. There was probably fear in them but that was not discernible from the upper floor. The tunnel had been sealed months earlier. Trucks and noisy workmen told us that. Lauman informed us, with notable pleasure, that he and a few guards had taken up residence nearby. That meant in Greta's place. It was depressing to think of those louts using her cherished home, eating at her table, relaxing in her chairs and sofas and whatever else.

Beck came in not long before the new year. He sat down on the settee and asked for tea. He made the request politely, almost humbly.

"It will be the tea made from nuts and roots, you know."

"That will be fine. I shall make a note to get you the real thing. Jasmine? Oolong?"

"We prefer the varieties found in England, though it seems unlikely you can get them just now."

Only after a moment did Beck get my meaning. Joshua smiled and took his tea to the backroom.

"I'll see what I can do. You would be surprised what I can find."

"You have not been here in quite a while, Herr Beck. Work must be pressing."

"Germany is alive! So much to be done. The German people are alive!"

"Most of them."

"More of your droll witticism. It would be best of you concentrated on fortune telling rather than comedy."

"I have many talents. And when can I expect to have more of your superiors gracing my parlor?"

"Things are falling into place for the next major effort. The officers mess is a beehive of activity and rumor. That means there will be people seeking your counsel – oh, and not your humor."

"They bring out my talents for parody and satire."

"Keep them hidden. They have talents too, of which you know only a small part. Bertha, my dear Bertha, you must know they do not like you or your people. I on the other hand see good things, if only occasionally. You must deliver the goods, as they say, or they will put you on a train."

"For Buchenwald."

"Probably Dachau. It's closer and efficiency is prized in Germany."

My wit flew away. My composure was not far behind. As much as I loathed the idea of showing vulnerability, I sobbed.

"Oh…. There is nothing more I can do. I am only following orders from on high. I wish I had been born far away from here. Or in a better time than the one we find ourselves in. I will leave you with one word. It is the code name for the coming war – *Barbarossa*."

I sensed sincerity and looked into his eyes pleadingly. I was sure of it. We had always needed one another: one of us for professional reasons, the other to stay alive. There was more now.

"You will have an important visitor next week. When I have a definite time, I shall let you know. No more escape attempts, eh Bertha? It would pain me to follow the order that would swiftly follow."

There were thousands of Becks in Germany then. They were everywhere - in train stations, bureaus, army installations, and perhaps even in the camps. I had a measure of compassion for only one of them though.

Beck informed me by courier that the important figure would call upon me the following evening. Joshua and I prepared the room and did our exercise routine. At the appointed time a Mercedes pulled up and a man disembarked from the backseat. It was not Hitler, Göring, or anyone else I had seen in the newspapers.

When he entered I could see he was a colonel. He wore an Iron Cross with the distinctive piping of general staff officers. His appearance suggested he was a career officer who aspired to great things.

He strode into the parlor, seated himself, and cocked an ankle on the other knee. No pleasantries. None of the "I have heard many good things about you" introductions. He was all business. I smelled brandy.

"Berlin has a formidable operation pending. It wants to know your thoughts."

His accent was from the south, not the Prussian east. By saying Berlin wanted my thoughts, he surely meant Hitler. I tried to read his eyes but saw only ice and documents and starch.

Boots sounding noisily in a long dark corridor. The footfalls echoed off the walls and merged with the sounds of a thousand typewriters.

He was not drunk, but he had had brandy not long ago. I closed my eyes and searched my mind.

"War in the east…much bloodshed…but much glory as well."

"And…." he said sternly.

"Much land will fall to Germany. A great deal of land. More than all Germany, more than what the Kaisers ruled."

"There must be more. Please tell me there's more."

"Alas, no. I cannot see details with any clarity and I do not guess."

He nodded slowly. His eyes turned down to my breasts and another form of attack and conquest crossed his mind.

"Most fortune tellers are rather plain. They use cosmetics to make themselves look exotic and enticing to their clients. You are quite beautiful. Naturally so. You don't mind my saying that."

My discomfort was clear. He reached across the table and placed his hand over mine.

"You know, I could help be of help to a woman like you. Surely, you feel that. Surely you know that."

He walked in a cat-like manner to behind me and caressed my shoulders.

"A woman whom men higher in rank than you consults is not in need of the help of a staff officer."

My condescension irked him and emboldened him. His hands moved down my arms and near my breasts.

"Perhaps it is I who can be of help to a clerk like you. It is only a matter of time until the Führer comes to see me again. I hope I am able to speak favorably of you, perhaps arranging a transfer."

His eyes flared. I thought he might strike me or worse but frustration set in and he grabbed his service cap and stormed out. He must have passed Beck outside. He surmised what had happened.

"Did he harm you?"

"He thought he could take advantage of me but he was badly mistaken."

"I see. Perhaps I should then ask if you harmed him."

"No, Reinhard. I acted with supreme restraint and even offered to have him transferred. Who was he?"

"He is in the Planning Division. Her serves on General Jodl's staff."

"Ah, just as I thought. Another clerk in a large soulless bureau."

"I will not dispute the assessment. I will try to be in attendance in future sessions with such dreary but rash functionaries. The higher ups I have less control over. And it is my duty to report that the head of all the functionaries and generals will seek your guidance within a month."

I shuddered.

Hitler arrived in the early evening after a stay in Berchtesgaden, though he hardly seemed rested after being at his mountain house. Perhaps he was just weary from the drive to Munich. He entered the parlor as his bodyguard detail stayed at the door. It was February 1941.

"You know me as a man of ambition. Everyone does now. Here and abroad, around the world. Yet I wonder how many of them can see the audacity of what I have planned. You sensed it. We know that. We also know your vision is not unlimited. What I need to know from you this night is what you see on the horizon now – many months after your first glimpse of my plan. I am certain you know more now. Tell me."

I sensed a deep prudishness about Hitler. He had a purity about him which wasn't based on morals but on insecurities and fear of perversity.

"I have indeed given the matter great consideration. I have immersed myself in the world that you and I know of, the world others do not see or believe in. You will drive deep into the enemy's heartland and you will be greeted in parts of it. Crowds will cheer you tanks and men."

He looked at me intently and saw my unease. He treasured it as his creation and as his method of gauging my reliability. Was it a matter of believing me or not, or killing me or not. I replied with steel-eyed determination.

"The plan is sound, the campaign will go well."

"Good. Good."

"Though there will be much blood and fire."

"Ahh…. I saw much of both in my youth."

"Your enemies will see much of both soon."

"We will see to that. Both will come in torrents! But you must tell me everything you see. Failure to do so will come at a price."

"The horizon has indeed moved forward as you so rightly said. It does not go on forever."

We stared at each other for a minute at least. I knew how to put an end to it.

"Bertha's word. Ah, forgive me, but this evening there is one more word – *Barbarossa*."

Hitler stifled a look of surprise, then nodded.

"Barbarossa. Amazing. It will go well. Good evening, Frau Bertha.

"Welcome to my parlor…" said the spider to the fly.

Yes, I had him on the hook alright. My satisfaction gave way as I saw more fires, cemeteries, blood, and trains – an endless line of trains. Each of his footfalls on my stairs was a death knell for millions.

Weeks passed. I had the guards bring me newspapers everyday but nothing was in print that Berlin did not want there and there was no word from the East. More time passed and unease set in. Did Hitler think I was lying? If so, the end was near. A few more weeks went by. In early April word came that the army had moved south into the Balkans and Greece. That made no sense to me but the newspapers said the move south was necessary to help Italy.

What would that mean for *Barbarossa*? It could mean the whole operation was canceled or put off for some time. If the latter, then for how long? Joshua and I wondered if I was still useful to the Nazis and it was increasingly clear that they had no use for Jews, except as slave laborers at Buchenwald, Dachau, and who knew how many other places.

One morning in June, the 22nd to be exact, the radio announced that the army had attacked the Soviet Union. There was the expected talk of the untrustworthiness of Stalin and the need to eradicate Bolshevism which in Nazi thinking was the creation of Jews. Over the next few days the broadcasts made it clear how enormous the campaign was. We listened to the BBC at low volume.

I knew nothing of the Red Army except that it was large and that Stalin had purged many generals a few years earlier. Well, Hitler had done the same thing with a handful of his generals so I envisioned a war led by many unqualified people. The broadcasts remained upbeat throughout the summer.

I was surprised they didn't move me to Berlin and keep me hidden away like a mistress in a Potsdam town house so that he could get readings from me at any time, day or night. Perhaps Hitler and his coterie thought word would seep out in Berlin. It was not that a gossipy media might get hold of the story, more that disloyal generals and party officials might find out. Or maybe he thought I operated best in my home, where I was comfortable. He did make occasional trips to his mountain retreat of Berchtesgaden and Munich was only 70 kilometers away. Anyway, I was glad to stay at home.

In August a few cars pulled up. From the window I saw a man spirited out of a Mercedes with a raincoat pulled high to cover his face, though there was no rain that evening. Hitler was calling on me and no warning had come from Beck or anyone.

"Shall I inform him we're not receiving guests just now and tomorrow would be more convenient?" Joshua impishly asked as he headed for the backroom.

"Go! Go! And not a peep out of you!"

You have no idea how repulsive a gleeful tyrant is. He sat at my table, again dressed in the brown, double-breasted suit, and leaned back in the chair.

"Your reading confirmed my judgment! Bah, those timid generals said we should never go or we should wait for next year! If we listened to them we'd be hiding along the old border lines, wringing our hands like children! Look at us now! We're at the gates of Moscow! Stalin and his Slavic hordes are on the run. More land for hearty German yeomen!"

I nodded and read his eyes and soul – as unpleasant an undertaking as I have ever done. There was hatred, derangement, narcissism, and above all, dilettantism. He made decisions based on the seat of his pants and gut instincts and could never be convinced he had erred. I nodded more.

"What can you tell me now? What do you see?"

I closed my eyes and drifted into the sea. I saw the same images of men, materiel, and trains. This time they were not moving, except for the trains. They were moving in another direction. I resorted to the device long used by soothsayers at traveling fairs: telling the client what he wanted to hear.

"I cannot see exceptionally far ahead in the great detail we would like. The drive is slowing down, though. Cold and snow are coming."

"And how long will this last!?"

"A few months at most. The trains are a problem. Too many trains in the way. Victory is not in doubt."

A moment of concern came across him. It quickly returned to ebullience and self-congratulation.

"Excellent! Invaluable counsel!" He turned to an aide and barked, "Have meals brought here from the Hofbräuhaus! And do not skimp on the wine!" He returned his attention to me. "Is French or German more to your liking?"

"German, of course." I hid my sarcasm as well as I hid my disdain.

Later that night, as Furtwängler performed Mozart on the radio, the guards brought over Bratwurst, Mettwurst, and Wiener Schnitzel. We were initially reluctant to trust the largesse of our earlier guest. What if he mistrusted me or felt he no longer needed a Jewish councillor? A moment's reflection told me that if either were the case he could have found a less delicate way of getting rid of us. I nodded to Joshua and we dug in. It was a rather heavy meal but a welcome one. We sat at the table as Gestapo hoodlums became dutiful waiters. One opened a bottle of Trollinger but did not know enough to allow Joshua to sniff the cork. Such gaucherie. I decided right then not to give him a tip.

The evening went well and as we finished our plumb crisps, I offered an unopened bottle of Trollinger to the waiters. They declined, but only after a moment of hesitation. Joshua placed it in one's hands and clasped his shoulder. Off he went down the stairs, his step a little livelier.

We sat in the parlor and listened to the BBC before retiring for the night.

"You know, Bertha, sometimes life is magnificently absurd."

"I quite agree. The most detestable man in Germany –"

"In the *world*."

"I stand corrected. The most detestable man in the world consults a Jewish woman about his plans to annihilate another country, then rewards her and her husband with a sumptuous repast."

"They left a huge rib roast in our icebox."

"We can have a few of them over for Shabbat then."

"Göring would devour the whole thing in one sitting, I fear."

We sat in silence for many moments and each of turned to more serious things.

"Just what do you see ahead, dear? Are they going to win this war as they think?"

"I cannot see the end with any certainty but I feel that the slowdown will prove very difficult. If they don't seize Moscow before the snows come, events will turn against them."

"That doesn't bode well for us."

We held each other warmly and in a few moments we kissed passionately. It might seem incongruous but amid the uncertainty of a world war it was important to find moments of personal assertion and intimacy. We could die tomorrow, so let's live this night.

That night I saw Joshua standing in the same corridor my father had stood in. I did not mention it to him in the morning.

Beck came for a visit in December 1941. His brow was furrowed. Events must have been weighing on him. We sat in the parlor, though there was no reading that day.

"Ach, Berlin is not a good place these days. Hitler is angry that the generals have not taken Moscow and Leningrad and the generals for their part feud with one another. Everyone remains confident that with warmer weather, in the spring, our panzers will roll again."

"But you, Reinhard, are not so confident."

"No, I am not. I have not been in the east. I am not a combat officer. However, I know many who are. Men I went through training with. Some I knew in my boyhood. I see them in Berlin. We talk – usually in low voices."

"They worry about the winter."

"The winter and the enemy. The Russians fight to the death. Some seem to die and rise up to fight us again, like Golem."

"This worries them."

"No, it does not. They remain, well, believers in the Reich, loyal soldiers of Adolf Hitler."

"Ah. So, Reinhard, it worries you then."

"It worried me a great deal. The men do not have winter clothing. The tanks cannot start up in the cold. It was that operation in the Balkans and Greece to save Mussolini. It threw off schedules and delayed Barbarossa for several months."

"For several warm months."

"What will happen, Bertha. You read the newspapers and then you have your gift. What is ahead for Germany?"

"I also studied history at the university, until Berlin deemed me unfit. One might have noted that Napoleon marched his army into Russia and even took control of Moscow but it burned down and he had to make a painful and disastrous retreat."

"Bertha my dear, I did not ask for a look into the past."

"I see dark events unfolding in Russia – and Poland too. I see blood, fire, mass graves and trains as far as the eye can see."

"And whither Germany?"

"The fire and smoke will consume the army – and Germany as well."

His face went blank. He leaned back in his chair in despair and nausea.

"You told me we would win and I can only presume you told Hitler the same."

"I said no such thing, Reinhard, neither to you nor to that Austrian wretch presently in Berlin."

"You said…. Ahhhh, you said victory was assured but you did not say which side would be the victor. You let us hear what we wanted to hear."

"Why, Reinhard. You missed your calling."

"There is plenty of that in the German government, I assure you. In any case, I foresee you will soon be visited by a disappointed high-ranking official in that government."

"A very high-ranking official."

"Yes. I further foresee you being less candid with him than you have just been with me."

"You indeed missed your calling. And for your information,

Joshua and I do not expect to live through this war. That in a way is a gift that allows us great freedom."

"Oh Bertha...."

The following morning cars arrived out front and I hied to the window to see the now familiar scene of Hitler with his collar turned up to cover his face heading for my doorway. The footfalls came less swiftly than before. In they came. Beck was with them.

"The war in the east has met with tremendous success, until recently. Did you not know of this when last we spoke? Answer me!"

"My senses are not attuned to the details of every arrow on big maps. Nor can exact dates be expected, though I did expect a firmer decision in the spring – and not months of delay. That I suspect was the result of generals – those men who obsess with small arrows on big maps."

Those words struck home. There was no doubt.

"Then the campaign will meet with success."

"Warmer weather brings new opportunities for greatness. I have always seen blood and victory for those who are not timid. Napoleon took Moscow and he had not one panzer or Stuka."

He smiled, ever so slightly bay he smiled. Whether it was my wit or a surge of narcissistic adrenaline, I know not. Or perhaps he suspected I was lying and had been for several months.

He signaled his retinue that it was time to go. He turned to me. His face was cold but nervous. I thought it might twitch.

"I rely on you, Frau Siegelman. All Germany relies on you. Do not let your Führer and nation down."

"Fate favors the valiant. Bertha's word."

I met his eyes unflinchingly and in silence from my chair. Beck was unnerved. Hitler turned and left. Joshua sallied forth from his backroom redoubt and stood behind me.

"I don't think he believed me, Joshua."

The news reports told of renewed efforts, especially in Moscow. Stalin had fled to parts unknown. The German army reached the outer areas of the capital but the Soviet army struck back and the German forces had to fall back. The radio said that Hitler was disappointed in his generals and sacked several of them. From now on, Berlin boasted, the war would be directed by the Führer himself.

Regular customers continued to come. Their requests were predictable and almost always the same. How will the war end? What about my son serving in Russia? I held their hands and saw flames and smoke. Most of their sons I saw done in by Russian troops or lying still on the frozen soil. Each time I did, I also saw the endless trains and vast graveyards and photographs of dead youths fluttering down from the sky. Naturally, I told them to keep up hope and await their loved one's return.

I couldn't do it anymore. I could no longer keep up pretenses. I could continue misleading Hitler and his minions; that served a purpose. But there was no purpose in lying to those poor mothers and fathers. The Reich deposited money in my bank regularly and Lauman and Beck would get me anything I wanted. I didn't need the money of those poor souls with sons in the war.

In early December, a day after the Japanese had attacked the US, Hitler arrived once more, this time accompanied by two generals and Beck. Hitler traipsed noisily into the parlor and shouted, "Get your husband out here!"

Joshua of course complied and stood near the window. A tirade erupted.

"My forces have been dealt a severe defeat – near Moscow and across the front. Heavy casualties! German troops in retreat! Unthinkable! Unimaginable! How do you explain this? You are supposed to know such things and report them to me accurately! Did you want me to fail? Did you play a Jewish ruse on me? Answer me! Or I will have you put to death this very hour."

He looked over to his officers. None of them was going to come to my defense, though Beck wanted to.

"I do not play ruses on people I work for. That would be bad for business and in the present case, it would be foolish. I am not a foolish woman. And killing me would take away an advantage you have over the enemies. That advantage is crucial in personal matters, business matters, and war and peace."

Again, we stared into each other. And again I was up to the task.

"Where have I misguided you? I foresaw success and in the end, great victory. You have won a tremendous victory and met with a setback. Alexander had setbacks. So did Frederick and Napoleon. They had nerves of steel and great perseverance. They are revered in history books the world over."

I was unable to gauge the faces of the generals, fixed as I was on the former corporal before me. However, I suspect that expertise in hiding emotions came with rising up the ranks and playing politics.

"It was the weather," he murmured. "The Russians are Slavs! They could never defeat my men."

He had found his own answer – one that suited his ego.

"Yes. The wretched weather. America has a warmer clime."

He froze.

"You see me invading America?"

"I see you declaring war on America."

He turned to the generals. "This woman thinks I am going to declare war on her fellow Jew, Franklin Rosenfeld!"

I took their unease and humor to mean that the idea had been discussed.

"And why would I declare war on America?"

"Because America is controlled by the Jews and the British and the Bolsheviks. War is only a matter of time. If you do to delayer war on Rosenfeld, as you call him, he will declare war on you."

"I have something in store for those Jews and British and Bolsheviks."

"More victory. More glory. Bertha's word."

Joshua and I were relieved when they traipsed out. I looked out see how much filth they had left on our Khamseh rug.

"Where do we stand, Bertha?"

"He has doubts but he remains on my hook."

"And his officers?"

"They think I'm hoodwinking him. No, they are sure of it, but they dare not say it to him."

"It seems the sane are against us and the madman is on our side."

"Such times, such times."

Life went on for Joshua and me. We rose every morning and have breakfast – rather decent ones for the time. Every few days we would draw up a list and Lauman would send a guard off to the marketplace. We even got a cache of real tea, not the ersatz stuff made from nuts and leaves and who knows what. There was our exercise regimen too. I tried to convince Lauman to let us walk to the park, under close watch, and he said he would look into it. A cheerful medium is a far-seeing medium, I told him.

I had nightmares most every night - the red fires, acrid smoke, and long trains. Every now and then they shocked me awake but more often than not I recognized them as annoyances, like noisy neighbors arguing into the night. I told Joshua that I had never had such dreams repeat themselves. He said I had never been imprisoned and visited by a madman before. I could not let go of a sense of unease though.

One day Lauman apologized for barging in, then abruptly took our radio. He said he was following orders. BBC news broadcasts had been an important source of hope for us. More importantly, they shaped what I told my august clients from Berlin. My prognostications were only partly drawn from the sea. They were equal parts inferences from the news and my studies of history while at university and what I thought would do the most damage. One of the pillars was now gone.

Lauman brought newspapers, which of course were propaganda, but the discerning reader can recognize overstatement, nonsense, and excuses and come to some understanding of what was really going on. The winter in Russia, for example, had been devastating and a new offensive was coming when spring came.

Oh, and Beck was a source as well. He worked and dined with

SS big shots and bloated, boastful wretches let things slip. Beck was increasingly disenchanted and talkative. He told me that the next offensive would not head for Moscow.

"Why not?"

"The capital is heavily defended, the south far less so."

"Is there anything there?" Joshua asked.

"Oh yes. Stalin's oil comes from the Caucasus. If we take that region, or sever it from the armies in the north, the bulk of the Red Army will be immobile."

"No tanks, no trucks, no war." Joshua said.

My feelings were that this new drive would be no more successful than the previous one, yet a sickening foreboding came over me. It seemed to emanate from Beck. He had not told all.

"What else have you come to tell us, Herr Beck?"

His eyes raced away from mine. He began to speak but could not.

"What is it?" I asked in a consoling voice I had never used with him before.

"The Reich is formulating an immense operation. It is almost as large as the war. It is a war within the war, one might say. There have been discussions underway for several years about what to do about what they call the 'Jewish Problem'."

Joshua and I fell silent. We had heard rumors but now we were getting intelligence.

"There were once plans to gather all Jews and send them out of Germany. One plan was sending them to Palestine, another to empty steppe land in Russia and Central Asia. Neither is feasible during the war and so the SS has decided on another solution. Jews – all of them – will be placed in camps where they will work in war industries. When they are no longer able to work, they will be killed. There are four camps set up in Poland that are designed to kill people by the thousands everyday. The camps are not large yet but they are being expanded rapidly. The materials are being sent and the labor is already there."

"All of them? All of the Jews?" Joshua asked incredulously. "Many are already in walled-up ghettoes."

"Yes, from all over Europe. They will be rounded up. The ghettoes were a first step. The solution is underway, gears are tuning, orders sent, trains are moving."

An endless train flashed before my eyes, leading to an immense inferno.

I saw a deeper evil in the Third Reich that evening. In the middle of an immense war with the Soviet Union, Britain, and the United States, the Nazis were embarking upon the annihilation of my people. Trains that could bring weapons to the fronts were being devoted to an act of madness.

"It will not be only Jews. Gypsies, communists, homosexuals, cripples – that are all to be killed."

"Women and children," I asked pointlessly.

"Yes. I believe the form of execution will be poison gas – a potent chemical called Zyklon B. Huge quantities are on order from IG Farben. The process will go on day and night. It's already underway."

"Whatever soulless people do this will themselves be put to death," I noted.

"That may be the case in coming years. For now, the killing goes on day and night, day and night."

Beck began to sob but his rank and upbringing demanded firmness. His back straightened as if called to attention by Bismarck himself.

I was convinced more than ever of the evil of that low-born churl from Vienna who sought my guidance. I dedicated myself to destroying him. I had no pistol. If I had I would gladly shoot him even though the consequences would be fearful. My weapons would be my knowledge of history, whatever information I could glean about the war, my guile, and my ability to read Hitler's mind. I wanted to know, as completely as I could, his concerns, fears, expectations. and narcissism.

Hitler came again in the early summer of 1942. He strode into the parlor and sat, perching a foot on the table, hand on chin, a passel of guards and hangers on in the anteroom. Confidence and cockiness emanated from him.

"You know why I am here. You need not have any exceptional skills to know that."

"I would be more able to serve you if I had a radio to listen to music and reports from Berlin. They support my exceptional skills."

"And reports from London. You need not have any exceptional skills to know that either. Now, on to your reading of things that concern me."

"Another drive has begun. This one is not directed at Moscow but to the south – to the Volga basin and the Caucasus. The capital is not as important as the oil from the south."

He paused. I believe he was startled. I opted to strike deeper.

"No tanks, no trucks, no war."

Something was racing through his head. Did I have a spy? Was I more gifted than anyone he had ever heard of? It was a combination of the two but I had no intention of telling him that. I stared intently into his eyes with the verisimilitude of mystery, then continued.

"There is an enormous loss of life, more than people can realize. I see fires and graves in the east as far as the eye can see. More than people can know, more than they want to know. Few can see the great, noble, patriotic purpose behind the loss of life. Only truly great men can see the purpose and understand its necessity for victory. I wonder if the knowledge lays heavy on the minds of the great men. Or if it is as light as a silk scarf and easily cast off."

That rattled him. He was unsure of my meaning and the extent of my knowledge.

"Those are questions best left to great men. The loss of millions of lives can be easily forgotten by people, all the more easily when they are enemies of good people. Now, Gypsy, what will the great, noble, patriotic effort in the east lead to."

"Though I see fires and graves as far as the eye can see, I cannot see the end, nor do I see the necessity. True courage is not about taking a life but to spare one."

"Do not lecture your Führer!"

"Victory is assured, as is your name in history books. Judgment will come."

He tried to piece what I said together and assess my intent. Our stares met and ended in stalemate. I saw rage flash through the soul of his night but never blinked.

"You know who developed the oil industry in the Caucasus, Gypsy?"

"The Rothschilds, of course."

"Of course you would know that. Of course, you would. Very clever. On with it then. Let me hear it." He motioned with his hand as he stood.

"Bertha's word."

"Always remember, Gypsy, that you are a poor Jew who serves at my discretion. That may have to be impressed upon you. *My* word! *Mine!*"

And down the steps they went. Car doors closed, an engine started, and the car sped away.

Joshua came slowly from the bedroom with a look of profound concern.

We were awakened by the dreadful sound of the door being shoved open and heavy boots coming down hard on the floor leading to our bedroom. Two men barged in, neither was a familiar guard.

Greta! Not again!

One of them was a junior officer in the SS.

"Joshua Siegelman, Stand up. I have orders to place you under arrest and take you into custody."

I screamed in protest and pulled my husband to me.

"This will only be temporary, dear. I'll be back home in a day or two. Be not afraid," he said soothingly but unconvincingly.

As they led him away, I called out, "If you harm him I will no longer provide my service to the Reich, including your Führer!"

The officer stopped cold. He was not concerned by my threat, he was insulted by it. He drew his pistol and shot Joshua in the head. My mind reeled and I swooned.

I came to, just when I do not know but it was late morning. I was lying on the couch and man in impeccable civilian garb was tending to me while a pair of guards stood by. I looked to the floor and saw a dark stain where Joshua had fallen. It was no dream. It was terribly real.

The doctor urged me to rest, left a small bottle of sedatives, and walked briskly past the guards.

Shortly thereafter, Beck entered, looked at the guards and me, and with genuine innocence asked what had taken place.

"Your people murdered my husband. That is what happened. Another page in the Reich's history."

His eyes came to the stain outside the doorway and knew the rest. He told the guards to wait downstairs and after demurral they complied down the steps.

"You two will burn in hell! I can tell you that!" I screamed in weakened voice.

"It was not on my order, I assure you. Nor was it Lauman's. It must have come from Berlin."

"Very high up in Berlin. Of that I have no doubt. Would that they shot me alongside my husband."

"I am so sorry for all this. Sorrier than I can ever express."

He helped me to my feet and fetched water and sedatives.

"Can you sleep in the parlor tonight?"

"Yes, of course."

In the morning he made breakfast and tea. Real tea.

I was deeply depressed for several weeks. I sat up in bed and only occasionally made the journey to the parlor. If a high-ranking Nazi had come, I might have rushed at him with a kitchen knife. I cared that little for my life and thirsted that much for immediate vengeance. It was not simply a case of melancholia following the death of a loved one. I was genuinely convinced that my death – my violent murder – was, if you will pardon the expression, in the cards. After a few days I reacquainted myself with my duty. I had to do it alone now.

Or so it seemed. Beck was apparently stationed in Munich and his visits became almost routine. Few were official. The conversation was light and intended chiefly to lift my spirits. In time they became friendly, then congenial, then comforting. I was isolated – no spouse, no friends, no radio. Just an occasional newspaper. It was he who opened up first.

His parents had died when he was only a boy. He had been quite close to his mother but his father was aloof and seldom home. His upbringing was in the hands of an uncle, an army officer and veteran of the trench warfare in the previous bloodletting, Boyhood was austere and conducive toward military life. When the SS was expanded he quit college and eagerly joined. What better way, he reasoned, to serve Germany and attain self-respect. His peers at cadet academy were filled with nationalism, youthful enthusiasm, and even idealism. I came to understand this position as I'd seen it in so many customers and people on the street. But understanding something is not the same as accepting or forgiving it.

Idealism gave way to soul-draining routines in camps and hunting down enemies of the state, as the Reich defined them. It was appalling how few of his fellow officers and troops felt the same. Most held fast to the ideology that Jews, homosexuals, and Gypsies were sub-humans whose existence weakened the Reich. Though he declined to spell out the nature of his work in the Abwehr I had no doubt it was related to surveillance and repression. He said he wished there was more he could do to change things. I told him he could help me. He looked at me in sorrow and hope.

An image went through my mind.

"Reinhard, do you have a brother?"

"Yes, I do. He is in the Wehrmacht, serving in Paulus's Sixth Army."

"And where are they now?"

"They are in southern Russia. From what I hear, they are nearing the Volga River."

Fire and ice, fire and ice.

I walked with him to the door and, unexpectedly, we embraced, my face pressing against his tunic. I know he had long had personal feelings toward me and now, despite the enormous chasm between us, I had feelings toward him.

"Ah, Bertha. I am trapped by this uniform."

"Your position can be of help. It already has been. You are my source of information. You are my BBC. My readings do not come solely from my inner ocean. They are built on reliable information I get from without."

Reinhard was startled, then pleased as he realized there was a small resistance movement in a Munich townhouse.

"Now, Reinhard, go home, go to the bureaus, go to Berlin. Talk, listen. Much more listening than talking, I suggest. And tell your friend in Munich what you learn."

I saw warmth I'd never seen before. He himself had probably not seen it in years or believed it to be still dwelling inside, like an ember beneath a pile of ash and dead wood. I considered asking him to communicate with his brother serving with Paulus but thought better of it. He would not be of much help in a few months.

Fire and ice, fire and ice.

MIRIAM ARRIVES

L oud boots coming up the steps. The door would swing open in any moment. An SS officer and three henchmen barged in, dragging an old woman. She was hurled to the floor. Her face showed signs of beatings and dried blood stained her tattered clothing – a cheap uniform of some sort. As she panted to regain awareness, her hollowed eyes and gaunt cheeks alarmed me. She looked at me with a sense of sorrow, not for herself but for me. The officer sneered as he spoke.

"This, Frau Siegelman, is Miriam Rosenstock. She is one of your people, though I am afraid there is no time for exchanges of family heritages and distant cousins and how you will celebrate the holidays."

"Have no worry about me," she said. "Whatever they do will be welcome."

He placed a Luger to the back of her head.

"Your cooperation with our officials is necessary. Any hesitation, demurral, or refusal will cost the life of Miriam here." He rubbed the pistol along her skull in almost tender way. "While she may mean something to you, she means nothing to me. And, Frau Siegelman, there are many more Miriams in Dachau. I see thousands of them in barracks, inspection yards, and trains. More are brought in every day. Your selfishness and lack of respect will cost them their lives – one by one, in their hundreds. Some not so swiftly as a bullet to the head. You will not be one of them. You will be kept alive, here, and given periodic reports on the number of deaths you have caused. Their fate is in your hands."

Rows of people, loudspeakers, trains.

Miriam and I looked into each other. I saw the horrors, the cruelty, and the degradation. I understood the system at work. And I at last understood the trains were not all bound for Russia.

"Death would be a relief," she whispered with considerable difficulty.

It would be – of that I was sure. Then there were the others. I recognized the situation.

"I will share my talents with the Reich on the condition that I be given periodic reports of this woman's condition. If she dies, I die. And your master will be displeased by his dog's misbehavior."

"You are a resourceful woman, Frau Siegelman. See that your talents do not fail her or you or *us*!"

"And Miriam stays here. Naturally, I do not want to burden the Reich with unnecessary lodging expenses."

He mulled it over briefly, then left.

Reinhard found a reason to come by every few evenings. He was thoughtful enough to dress in civilian garb and he made dinner for us once or twice – beef and potatoes, nothing fancier. Let us say the meal was not up to Hofbräuhaus standards but it was appreciated, nonetheless. Meat was becoming scarce for most people.

Afterward we sat in the parlor and tried desperately to have conversations. Around all Germany families and friends gathered and spoke of the war and work and the men who were running Germany. That was not the case in my home. We spoke of the weather and parks and great events from our childhoods. Miriam retired to the guest room, leaving Reinhard and me.

"The war in Russia continues to do well, though supply lines are long and constantly under attack by partisans. Unless we inflict a serious defeat in a few months, the winter will shut the drive down once more."

"What of the western front? America will come calling soon."

"Hitler believes the U-Boats can keep the Americans at bay. The consensus in the officer messes I frequent is that Americans will invade North Africa later this years, imperiling Rommel and the forces there."

"Defeat in the deserts and stalemate in the steppes. Does this mean the tide will turn?"

"That, Bertha, is your calling, not mine."

"Oh, Reinhard…."

"Wars depend on supplies of men and materiel. The United States and Soviet Union have more than we do – far more. Our troops can fight hard and long but the other side is simply too strong."

"Then it's a matter of momentum. An object expends its energy, comes to halt, then is pushed backward by an object with more energy."

"By an object with more planes, tanks, men, and –"

"And with saner leadership. Good evening, Reinhard. Thank you for dinner."

"You're welcome. Both of you. There is one thing…. Could you explain to Miriam how terrible I feel about this? I feel as though I am living with a curse haunting me. I want it to be over."

"I will do that as best I can though I cannot promise anything. May I ask one more thing? What is the name of the Soviet general in the south?"

"Oh, let me see. That would be Zhukov. Georgy Konstantinovich Zhukov. He's from a town just outside Moscow. We occupied it briefly in late 1941."

Living alone in something like solitary confinement was awful. Every step I took echoed off the plaster wall and reminded me of Joshua. So did the stains on the oak floor where he and Greta died. I was descending into a form of madness, I am sure of it. Humans are simply not intended to be without loved ones and neighbors. There was a fellowship with people at marketplaces and train stations and parks that goes unappreciated. I had none of that.

Miriam was a godsend. I was no longer isolated. I helped her back to health and put her in some of my clothes which I no longer used for social gatherings and evenings on the town. The fit was quite loose owing to malnutrition and beatings. After a few weeks her health was returning and I had an exercise partner again and an excellent conversationalist too.

She knew how dark the Reich's heart was from months at Dachau and a sub-camp. She spoke of hard work and meager meals, usually a morsel of rye and half-liter of thin soup. Guards were brutal and unrestrained my laws to rules. The camp's purpose was to extract labor from inmates, usually in some sort of war production, and let them die from malnutrition, beatings, or disease. More came in.

Death came in other, distinctive ways. Some inmates were sent to buildings where cruel medical experiments were performed on them, including submersion into icy water and confinement to a low air pressure chamber. Many were sent, few returned.

Every week inmates were assembled in a yard for "selection". Those deemed healthy enough to work, stayed on. The others were herded onto trains bound for Poland. Dachau guards were overheard gloating that the unfortunate souls were put to death by the thousands, though the circumstances were unclear.

She spoke at length and in great pain of one incident she witnessed.

"We were being transported form Dachau to a sub-camp that was many kilometers away. The truck stopped and I could see several dozen people – men, women, children – standing in a field, surrounded by SS guards. I could identify fathers and mothers clutching their children. Most of them were weeping. An old woman held a child and sang as the parents looked on. Another man held a child and pointed to the sky.

"The guards paced slowly around them, weapons at the ready. Some had cigarettes and seemed bored. An officer barked an order and the guards placed the poor souls in rows. Only then did I see a pit behind them. The machine guns did their job. Another row was set up, then another, then another. It went on for half an hour."

"Why, Miriam?"

"Why any of this? I never knew. Someone on the truck said it might have been a reprisal for an escape. Or perhaps Dachau was fully booked that day. There were occasional trainloads of Russian prisoners."

"Russian prisoners! They brought them to southern Germany? Why?"

"They were put to work like the rest of us. At least at first. I spoke with a few in the evening before we were locked into the blocks and at the selection yards. Some spoke German. The Reich's troops were slaughtering Russians, soldiers and civilians alike. They said no Russian would sleep until every German was dead or driven out. I never saw such ferocity in a man's eyes."

"You said they were put to work 'at first'."

"One day hundreds of them were taken from the selection yard. They were in good health but they were separated from the healthy. The faces of the guards told the tale. The Russians were marched out, looks of resignation on their faces. An hour later, while at work, we heard the rattle of machine guns. The same tragedy played out the next day and the next."

Miriam counted herself as fortunate, all things considered. Her health was good, despite the recent beating, and her work was indoors at sewing station where uniforms were made. The *Aufseherinnen* who watched us at work were less harsh than the guards. Production quotas had to be made, you know. She and her husband were separated on arrival and she had no idea where he was. An informal network arose trying to communicate with loved ones somewhere in the sprawling Dachau system but there was no word of him.

She had taught literature at the gymnasium level and enjoyed the writings of Heine and Schiller. She was also conversant in the thought of Fichte and Kant. We wondered what had happened to Germany and never arrived at any real answer. Future historians would have to work that out. The more important question was how long would Germany be like this and what was coming.

I eventually told her of my gift and my distinctive clients from Berlin – one who came by way of Austria."

"So that's how I came to be sent to you. Strange but wonderful. I am here with Hitler's mystic. Will you forgive me if I stay in the backroom on his next visit?"

"Ha! That would be for the best!"

THE HEART OF EVIL

The Austrian corporal arrived a few weeks later. He was in a pleasant mood. He asked if the guards were keeping the pantry well stocked and if I felt safe. He sat at the table, cocked a foot on a knee and bade me to sit.

"Go into it. Go into your state of mind."

"I shall. I know what you want know."

I also know what you want to hear.

Images of death, sharpened by Miriam's accounts, intermixed with feelings from the sea and haunted my nights. The images were all the more revulsive at the table just then.

"The effort in the east is costing millions of lives. Not all of the deaths are needed. Some result from incompetence and poor advice."

"Whose incompetence. Whose poor advice."

I stared into him and replied, "Precisely who is something you can discern far better than I. The humble seer sitting before you knows the situation and environment. The details are illusive, hazy at best, and unrecognizable from here. But there is no mistaking the matter. None!"

He mulled it over. I had struck something inside him.

"Less on the war in Berlin and more on the one in Russia, if you please."

"The Americans understand vast open regions. We in Germany know dark forests."

He again thought my words through and saw them as praise for the mythic Teutonic past.

"The east now, if you please."

"The fires and smoke and graves go on to the horizon. And at the risk of displeasing my esteemed guest, not all of the deaths are needed."

A sense of his hatred of the Soviet Union and Joseph Stalin swept through me – intense, unreasoning hatred, though alloyed with a boundless narcissism. His magnificence would be proven to all by his mastery of what he hated.

"Nevertheless, you must go deeper into the heart of evil."

His stare intensified. I think he read my perceptions.

"Yes, yes. The end, if you please. The end! Out with it!"

"The noblest struggles are long and painful. Siegfried knew that. Frederick knew that. The German people know it as well. They deserve more skillful and daring leadership as they tear at the heart of the enemy."

"And where is the enemy's heart?"

"The heart beats in the city that bears the name Stalin."

That too resonated inside him. We stared into each other's souls. I did so with more confidence than ever before.

"The heart beats in the city that bears the name Stalin. Cut it out and hold it up to the heavens as proof of who you are. Bertha's word."

"Yes, it is." He stood abruptly and his retinue opened the door and prepared the way to the car. "Ahh, there is something else. Speak!"

"There is one more word before you leave. That word is… Hofbräuhaus."

He looked back to me, amused by the impertinence. After a sneering chuckle, he told an officer to see to it.

MIRIAM'S WORDS

We dined that night on an excellent rib roast with red wine. The whole thing caused Miriam to shake her head in disbelief. My audacity stemmed from a desire to get her back to good health – to reverse what those view hoodlums had done to her. Over the weeks she regained weight and color returned to her face and hands. The darkness in her soul would never go away.

She mentioned a daughter but when my look urged her to go on, she fell silent.

She asked for pen and paper. I thought she might want to put down in words what she had been through in Dachau but she wanted nothing to do with that, at least not then. She wrote a poem. I loved it and committed it to memory.

Imagine to yourself

Imagine a beautiful world,
Less sad than it is.
We go there with light in our pockets,
Above rooftops and the stars,
As time passes without fear,
I'm going to be there in heaven.

Imagine some happiness,
Because it's so rare here,
A place with no darkness,
And you are in the middle of a beautiful day,
Heaven above you, and love all around you,
A simple world with reflections of lights and joy,

But all humans have left,
And a blanket of darkness has fallen,
There is no difference between days and nights,
And there is nothing to imagine,
No blue skies, no dazzling sun,
I'm going to see it all in heaven.

I am on my way.

STALINGRAD

The little dictator came calling in late 1942. A major battle was underway at a city on the Volga that Stalin bestowed his name upon. I had been thinking over what the newspapers, Beck, and Miriam had said and their words intermingled with senses I had in the sea. As much as I wanted the Reich to destroy itself in the Soviet Union I felt the war would go on and it would be best if I added nuance to my readings. It would bolster his confidence in me and ensure the path to ruin.

He sat at the table in his usual cocky pose and ran down his great accomplishments against Stalin. He was confident. The Soviet forces were falling back and suffering extraordinary casualties.

"The Ivans have taken a beating and falling back. We have better tanks and planes coming in the spring. The war will be over next year. That is clear. What say you, Gypsy?"

I met his stare and held it, allowing a trace of concern then sorrow come across my face.

"The steppes extend across the Ukraine almost to China. I see such ferocity in the faces of Russian soldiers. There are many of them. They will strike back. They know winter as well as the Americans know deserts. Such fires, such ice."

He was disappointed. Ire flashed in his eyes for a moment.

"And what should I do then, Gypsy? Toss my saber to Stalin and flee to the Netherlands?"

"You are heading into Stalingrad. It will be a mass grave for many brave Germans."

"You did not answer my question," he said with gritted teeth.

"Stalingrad…mass grave. Stalingrad…mass grave."

He stood up angrily and paced around the room, his retinue greatly concerned.

"A mass grave? For Stalin, not me!"

"I see great agony there. Beware Zhukov."

"Zhukov is a peasant! Stalingrad will be mine! Mine! Mine!"

"Mass grave…. Bertha's word."

He fell silent, then headed for the door and noisily descended the stairs.

Shortly later three guards barged in and beat me. The details are unpleasant to recount but suffice to say they were not hitting as hard as they could and that was clearly on orders. It was Miriam who tended to *me* this time. I composed myself and sat with her before bedtime.

"What if you are wrong, Bertha?"

"The battle for Stalingrad will be long and bloody. That's really all I said. If he takes Stalingrad it will be very costly and the war will continue. If he falls back it will nevertheless be costly and the war will drag on. Either way, Bertha's word will be essentially correct – fire and ice, mass graves. No victory for the swine."

"And your sage counsel will still be sought, more than ever."

"Probably so. Beck has a brother at Stalingrad."

"Poor boy…. Odd that I feel concern for German soldiers after what one did to my daughter."

I leaned forward with a sense of foreboding.

"My husband and I had a daughter, a child named Sonia. She was lovely and intelligent. She was about twenty-five when they came to march us to the Stuttgart rail station and pack us into trains for Dachau."

"Miriam, if this is too painful…."

"No, I want to tell you. I want to say what happened to Sonia. One of the SS men was obviously attracted by her and tried to take her into the bedroom. When we protested he threatened to kill us all on the spot. My husband and I stood helplessly. We heard her scream and the sickening sounds of rape. Then there was a shot. Yes, having had his way with her, he killed her. Numb, we marched to the rail yard and crammed into the train. I never saw my husband again. As I sewed uniforms at Dachau I thought of my little girl. I came to believe she was in a better place."

"Yet you have sympathy for Beck's brother."

"He is just a boy with a sense of duty. I was taught to avoid hatred, it blackened the soul." An idea came across her. "Bertha, you have remarkable gifts. That is clear. You can focus your mind and see what is to come. Have you ever thought you have other powers in your mind?"

"What do you mean, dear?"

"What I mean is maybe you can concentrate on killing someone and in so doing, he will have a heart attack or burst into flame."

"Or a Valkyrie will carry him off? Miriam, the thought has occurred to me and I have searched my entire being for that power. If I had it I would have deployed it with all my might on that monster who comes here periodically."

That wasn't true. I had swum on the sea toward where that gleaming power lay in the dark distance but became frightened and turned back.

I moved deeper and deeper into the flames in the east, along straight railroad tracks, past row after row of dark buildings, thick clouds of gas and mass graves. Huge hosts of soldiers were being devoured by an angry, merciless red giant. Letters flittered down from the sky in their millions before bursting into flashes of light and smoke. Darkness lifted revealing children dancing in a fountain surrounded by rubble. The giant stood quietly above them in the distance.

FAITH AND DISQUIET

A handful of high-ranking Wehrmacht officers came to me, escorted by Reinhard. That was comforting as I did not trust dutiful officers to maintain their comportment given how the war was going. Reinhard would protect me if he could, though I sensed deep sadness in him despite an official demeanor.

A young thin general sat at the table while rest stood in the background. He did not have the appearance of a starchy Prussian and when he spoke his Swabian accent supported my judgment, even though he spoke in low tones.

"Certain events have not played out as expected."

"You speak of Stalingrad," I replied. "Paulus surrendered. There were some who say it did indeed play out as expected."

He was surprised by my bluntness, though I was not sure he knew of my warning to his Führer. I sensed the name of the Russian city stabbed Reinhard.

"Perhaps, perhaps. However, I am not here to look over the past. Warm weather is here and new forces are ready for another offensive. The planning is much more careful. Berlin is confident and so are his generals."

"All of them, you say."

"Yes, all of them! Now, what of the spring offensive? What do you see?"

"I have given the war in the east a great deal of thought. I have peered into the mists as best I can. I continue seeing flame and smoke. The first two efforts have fallen short. There is no sign this one will meet with greater success."

He remained silent, then spoke more softly than before.

"And why is that?"

"There is too much faithlessness in Berlin. Besides, the Reich is wasteful and cruel, needlessly so. Not only on the fronts but behind them as well – in Poland and in places here in Germany as well."

"These are not the earnest words of a seer! They are the foul lies of a Jew!"

"Nothing is to be gained in wrath, neither in Russia nor in my dwelling. Russia has been a failure, has it not?" He did not give an answer, I did not need one. "There are many generals who know the truth, are there not?"

"The Führer is confident in final victory and so are we all."

I sensed he was lying. There was considerable disquiet in his caste.

"Then millions will die. In Russia, Poland, and north of here."

He stood abruptly and raised his hand to me.

"Halt!" Reinhard shouted. "The Führer asks for her honest readings. There will be no harm done to her!"

Reinhard was outranked but the regular army feared the SS. And of course Reinhard suggested that Hitler wanted me unharmed. That was ridiculous but I neglected to tell the general that.

"The Führer is adamant. I remain loyal to him. Do you have anything more for me?"

"There is nothing more for you here. Russia awaits…. Bertha's word."

He looked stricken, doomed. He left with the others. Reinhard sat down at the table and Miriam quietly joined us.

"Russia is an obsession with Hitler, my dear ladies. He will not heed your advice, unless it is what he wants to hear."

"An occupational hazard. What of his generals, Reinhard? What do they think of the Austrian corporal now?"

"There are whispers. I hear them only indirectly as my personal contact with Hitler is known. This year's offensive will be crucial. If it fails and the allies invade France early next year, the whispers will be more numerous and more daring."

"Or more desperate," said Miriam.

"There was an uprising in Warsaw. The Jews of northern Poland were crammed in to a decrepit part of the city. They smuggled weapons in and revolted. It had taken weeks to contain it. The fighting has been snuffed out."

"Jews and Russians will bring down the Reich," Miriam said with a hope I had not seen.

"Reinhard," I said, "what do you know of your brother? He was at Stalingrad."

"No word. Paulus and 90,000 soldiers surrendered. I fear the worst. Bertha, can you...."

"I have, Reinhard. Of course, I have. I am sorry. There is only darkness."

He nodded solemnly and almost teared up.

"Death is all around me. How long will the war last?" he asked.

"At least two years."

"We must find ways to stay alive until then."

Miriam sighed and excused herself.

A LITTLE FREEDOM

Miriam was not doing well. She was depressed, her appetite fell, and my dresses were once again drooping over her frame. She stayed in the backroom and only came out for meals and even then she had to be coaxed. At nights I heard sobbing and sometimes a piercing scream. She kept asking me to search my being for the power to kill Hitler and I repeated my inability to find it.

I told Lauman, the guard officer, that my health was deteriorating from being cooped up. I demanded that Miriam and I be allowed to take walks and go shopping. I added that we fully expected him to provide "chaperones", which made him chuckle. My request went up the chain of command and in a few days, to my delight, it was approved. I then said we would naturally need money for groceries and necessities. He handed me an envelope with a hundred Reichsmarks – a tidy sum.

So off Miriam and I went to the grocers, a flower shop, and a clothing store – our chaperones never far behind. Had we made a dash for it, would they have shot us? I doubt it. They could have run us down in ten seconds. Consumer goods were not in good supply of course but it was nonetheless a wonderful break from the tedium. Afterwards we went to the park and enjoyed the sun and fresh air.

People were not as lively as they were a few years earlier. People gazed ahead blankly or looked at photographs from their purses . How many of them had loved ones in the army? How many had loved ones in a mass grave somewhere?

Allied bombers were making themselves known to German cities. We could hear the wail of sirens and the thuds of antiaircraft guns and bombs in the distance. They would get closer. We passed houses that I knew had been the dwellings of Jews and it was clear there were new residents. God help the old ones. God help them.

Upon returning from one outing we came upon Reinhard waiting outside. He came upstairs and Miriam headed to the backroom. Reinhard and I sat on the settee.

"Even the newspapers are talking of a long war," I said.

"So is everyone in Berlin, except for a few sycophants. Italy has become problem. Mussolini is unnerved and his army is nearing collapse. The debate is whether to pull out of Italy and use the Alps as a defense or to fight in Italy and keep the government on our side."

"What do you think Berlin will do?"

"I cannot be sure. But I think Italy is a lost cause and the army has more pressing concerns in Russia. And of course the US and Britain will invade France next year."

"My concern is that Hitler will suddenly throw a tantrum and have me shot or hanged or beheaded."

"The guillotines in the cities are busy, mostly with routine criminals. Those who incur the state's wrath suffer crueler departures from this life. There's no doubt of that. Worry not, Bertha, you remain useful. You are protected. Those guards are down there to keep you from running off but they are also there to protect you."

"They are of help against routine criminals. They can be of no help against the bigger ones."

"I wonder what will befall me after the war. You are a fortune teller, not part of the Reich. I on the other hand wear its uniform and do its bidding. The allies will treat harshly with me. I may rot in a Siberian prison camp. I can only hope that my brother survived Stalingrad and is a prisoner of war somewhere."

Sorrow fell across his face like a cloud upon a sunny field. Pensiveness and anger then made their presence.

I saw him sitting alone with a pistol.

"After Stalingrad was encircled and the effort to lift the siege failed, the army allowed soldiers to write letters to their families. They were packed up and loaded onto aircraft which would fly out of the doomed city."

"A humane gesture amid an immense tragedy."

"The letters never arrived. The planes lifted off and made their way to our lines and then on to Berlin. But the letters never reached loved ones. They were never intended to reach loved ones. The generals used the letters to get an idea of the morale inside Stalingrad, then used the information to bolster morale in the public, probably by selecting patriotic letters and ignoring gloomy ones, or burning them. This is the army, not the party. I would have hoped for more from the generals. They have enjoyed so many privileges from Germany that they owe the nation more."

Reinhard reached into his coat and handed me a single pink rose.

"Why, Reinhard, what a kind gesture."

"We must make and appreciate such gestures to keep our humanity."

He pressed his lips to mine and I met them, willingly though not completely. After several moments I pulled back. I admit it was a lovely moment but it could not grow into a more passionate one. I still thought of myself as a married woman. Nonetheless, Reinhard and I were on a certain path.

"There is nothing more in the world that I would want than your love, Bertha. I need..."

"To feel more human."

"More human, and less guilty."

MIRIAM'S REVENGE

By July of 1943 the war in Russia was dragging on. The annual offensive had done well initially. The previous ones had shown promise too but they both stalled. This one I sensed would be the last. As it turned out, Zhukov blunted the drive and launched a powerful counterattack. The war would continue but exhaustion and uncertainty were clear. I read it in the repetitive phrases in the newspapers and saw it on the faces of people in the streets.

Then there was the allied invasion of Italy. I saw trains diverted south. The Reich was finished but it did not realize it yet, if it had, it would be all the more dangerous at home.

I did not hear from Herr Hitler during the turn of events. That was a welcome surprise for which I was grateful. I was, however, visited by a pair from Berlin. One an SS colonel, the other a civilian. We sat at the table.

"The Reich is embarking on a change of course in the south and your views on the policy are called for in the highest echelon."

The two men were clearly of lower stations in German society. That was clear from their accents, demeanor, and what I read from their presence.

"You are speaking of Italy."

The civilian nodded.

"You are displeased with an ally's leadership...and wish to shift support to another man, a general. Or abandon your ally altogether."

They both nodded and struggled to avoid looking at each other to gauge the other's reaction. I sensed a policy had been already decided upon and the humble seer of Munich was simply expected to ratify it. I knew that North Africa had been lost, Sicily too, and the western allies would be invading Italy any day, then France.

"Abandoning one man is more valuable than abandoning a whole nation."

With that I hoped they would squander men and materiel in Italy rather than use them elsewhere. I stood and began to lead them to the door when Miriam raced from the backroom, knife in hand, and stabbed the officer several times before he drew his pistol and shot her before he collapsed and lost consciousness.

Miriam seemed content as she passed away, pleased that she had killed at least one of the bastards. I kissed her forehead and recited the Kaddish over her.

The civilian had raced downstairs and was returning with Lauman and a guard. They pressed cloths on the officer's wounds and took him away. I cannot be sure of his fate. However, had he died from the stabbing there would have been a crush of Gestapo and SS goons rummaging about, demanding questions, and making threats. As it turned out there was none. Lauman arranged for Miriam's remains to be taken away a day later.

BUCHENWALD

Reinhard arrived a few days later. Two guards came with him but stayed outside. His anxiety was as ill an omen as I had seen. It took several moments for him to get it out.

"Bertha, I am afraid I bear bad news this day. It comes from higher up. Probably very high up. It has been decided that you must leave your residence here and be transported elsewhere."

"To Berlin, I suspect." I imagined that Hitler wanted me closer to hand. My gift failed me at that moment, however.

"I'm afraid not. You will be sent to a place about 150 kilometers southwest of the capital – Buchenwald."

"Buchenwald!"

The name shocked me. I knew it to be one of the notorious SS camps where people were starved and worked to death. Had my ruse with the Führer been found out? Was I being punished for my impertinence? Was it Miriam's knife attack?

"So I am marked for death then."

"No, not at all. Had you been so marked there would have been no apologetic visit from me. You would have been whisked off to an executioner or packed into train for Auschwitz. I was able to persuade Berlin that you might still be of service, especially in a more convenient setting, less than genteel though it is."

"Were you at Buchenwald at some point?"

"Yes, I was several years ago as it was used for people suspected of sedition. I am not unfamiliar with the staff there now. The commandant is a boorish fellow named Koch and I have made it clear to him and his lieutenants that you, having served the Führer himself, will be assigned only light duties. Berlin views your presence there as a way of threatening you: perform your work well for the Reich or you will be treated as a regular inmate and endure far worse. I see another dimension." His tone shifted from cold officiousness to warmth. "Bertha, I can watch over you, protect you from guards, and see that you are better fed."

"Will I have a valet?"

"Bertha, Bertha, your humor is misplaced and poorly timed. Buchenwald is a dreadful place and parts of the medical building are the worst. I hope your stay will be a brief one and I can get you back here after, oh, a period of time."

So, I was still useful to the Reich. That was a relief. I packed a valise and walked downstairs with Reinhard to his staff car.

"I would open the door for you, Bertha, but the neighbors might talk."

"Misplaced and poorly timed."

We drove north on the Reich's famed Autobahn system and passed military convoys and streams of trucks busily shipping war material. Near Regensburg there were yawning craters in farm fields and damaged buildings in the distance.

"Allied bombers," Reinhard said. "There are Messerschmitt factories here. They are mostly underground though."

As we continued farther north we came upon the wreckage of several allied planes.

We exited the Autobahn and drove east through farm fields and forests and small villages. The word "picturesque" might have occurred to other travelers in other times. Soon enough there were rows of barbed wire and guard towers. Soldiers with dogs patrolled the perimeter. Reinhard spoke with the guards at the checkpoint and we drove under a black gate with *Jedem das Seine* fashioned into the wrought iron. That meant «To Each What He Deserves".

We passed rows of factory where Reinhard said rifles, mortars, and machine guns were manufactured, using slave labor of course.

On the other side was a large field where thousands of poor soul were lined up with guards with machine pistols around them. We arrived at several barracks designated a medical section. When the car door opened a foul stench, something like raw sewage, struck me. A handful of male inmates in striped uniforms were making repairs to the buildings and grounds.

"The perimeter wire is electrified. The current is sufficient to cause death."

"What goes on here, Reinhard. I suspect the term 'experiments' is a euphemism."

"Yes, it is. I shall spare you the more unpleasant details but at present the Reich is interested in research on typhus. It strikes troops very hard at times and Berlin wants a vaccine."

Reinhard and I went to a back building where a young waif in a gray uniform led us to a backroom.

"Is she my valet?" I whispered.

Reinhard, in full uniform and imposing voice, told the nurse, "This is a special resident who has done services for high officials in Berlin. They want her treated well here and not to be part of or witness to the experiments. Meals will be brought to her and her laundry will be done regularly and correctly. Under no circumstances are any personnel to come here without my approval. I will repeat my instructions to Commandant Koch this evening at the officers mess, though of course we both know that that is a mere formality."

Reinhard bade me farewell. He wanted to do more but that was out of the question. I sat on the bed and heard the door lock. The room was about five meters by five meters, flat white paint, a single bed, and a small night stand. Toilet facilities were included. A small sooty window offered a little sunlight and a cheerless view of institutional facilities and weary, grimy laborers.

I had been confined in my townhouse for over a year but it was mine. It was my home. My table, my curtains, my bedroom, my view. This was a room in a penal colony, where most had committed no crime. They were Jews, homosexuals, political opponents, and anyone who ran afoul of Berlin. There were also Russian prisoners.

I saw boys and girls no more that twelve. They were in a hell, I was in a purgatory with a view of hell. Throughout the night I heard occasional screams. Some of pain, some of helpless outrage. Men, women, and children. I felt anxiety, fear, and despair. I lay down as darkness fell and wept. I wept for those poor people in Buchenwald, and those in Dachau, Auschwitz, and all the places I did not know about but sensed stretching across Europe, especially in the blazing east.

The young woman brought me a meal at dusk. Loudspeakers called out orders to those in the assembly yard, then played a Beethoven piano concerto.

"Strange," she said. "Hearing such lovely music in an abyss."

"It certainly is. Your name?"

She looked away suddenly.

A dozen inmates traipsed past the window, a well-armed guard behind them, occasionally shoving, always glaring.

"They're new arrivals. They'll be used to develop a typhus vaccine by being exposed to typhus from vials stored here. Some will live, most will not. If not from typhus then from diphtheria, cholera, various infections, and malnutrition."

"But there will be more new arrivals."

"Exactly. In a week. Sooner perhaps."

The staccato sound of gunfire came from a hundred meters or so away.

"I cannot say what that was. Punishment, sport, warning."

Was she a nurse or an inmate? I thought the latter. Heavy boots were coming down the hallway. An SS officer stood in the doorway.

"I am Sturmbannführer Hanke. Welcome to Buchenwald," he said coldly if not menacingly. "You will be under my direction at all times. A uniform will be brought to you and tomorrow you will take your place in one of our factories. You will follow my orders and those of other camp officers, guards, and *Aufseherin*. You will be an inmate here, save for your nights which will be spent here."

I tried to comprehend this man but I could not get past his cold demeanor and penchant for rules and authority. There might not have been anything else to him. He was what the Reich had wanted and created and recruited and mass produced – obedient functionaries with a modicum of competence.

"Have I made myself clear, Frau *Siegelman*?"

"Ja *wohl*."

I refrained from clicking my boots.

"I am sure that you will learn a great deal from your stay in our camp."

"It will be a singular experience. Of that I am sure."

He left and I remained in my austere room alone. I crawled into the bed. The sheets were clean and crisp and reeked of disinfectant. I lay down and took in the essence of Buchenwald – cruelty, exploitation, bureaucratic machinery. Gears set into motion for many years from wretches in Berlin were grinding people into dust.

Despite Reinhard's assurances I could not be sure I would not be one of them. My sleep was haunted by fire and smoke and immense trains hauling loads of lost souls.

I awoke to the sound of marching feet, angry shouts, and classical music. It was the same Beethoven piece. The young woman came with a tray of food. She knocked first.

"Fresh from the officers mess hall." A glimmer of pleasantness came across her weary face. "Their food is much better than what the guards get and as for us, oh, we get a morsel of bread and a half-liter of gruel."

I hesitated to partake.

"Eat. Whether you feel like eating it or not you have to eat. You will need the energy at the factory. An *Aufseherin* will be here shortly for you. Have courage."

I heeded her advice and pecked at the sausage, potato, and egg. It wasn't bad but it was not up to Hofbräuhaus standards. Nor was it kosher. I sat on the bed peering out the sooty window on the cruel regimen imposed on people. The *Aufseherin* walked in and tossed a pile of clothing onto my lap.

"Put them on, now, and then we are off to your work station."

It was a thick gray dress with oddly oversized collar and buttons running down to the waist. The fabric was coarse and scratchy and I knew it would chafe despite being too large for me, however the matron did not appear amenable to fetching me better attire from Buchenwald's couturier. Nor did she seem amenable to giving me privacy while I changed. She tossed down wooden clogs. The young woman inmate arrived with a bowl, spoon, and cup. They were not new or even clean.

The previous owner died a few days ago.

"Watch over them. They are often stolen and we do not issue replacements for the careless."

"And so I shall. Where may I wash them?"

"At the dining hall. We are going there now."

I thought it best not to mention my earlier meal. We walked along a muddy path past crowds of sickly men who had strangely determined faces.

"Russian prisoners," my guide said. "They don't last long."

"They know it."

My clogs stuck in the foul-smelling mud which had signs of vomit and feces. There were no dogs in sight. A line of women stood in front of the mess hall. Their hair shorn, their faces marred by grime, hunger, and resignation. My *Aufseherin* escort took me past the lines and into a hall with long wooden tables. To the side were faucets and basins but most of those who just came in went straight for the food which consisted of porridge, bread, and tea. I took my portions and sat next to a young women who recognized me as a newcomer.

"You have to learn to eat whatever there is. It can make all the difference at the next selection."

I knew that term from Miriam. Raise your arms and cough, this line or that line, life or death. I let her have my porridge.

"Hurry! Roll call soon," she said. "There are only a few hundred women here so it goes quickly. The men have it worse."

I washed my belongings and went off to the assembly yard, the

Aufseherin just behind me. Guards made a headcount and names were called. My escort approached me.

"You are not on the manifest but they know of you. Join the other women and go to the factory. I will come to take you back to your room after the evening meal."

Off we went to a row of drab factory buildings, a procession of hopeless women. An older woman took me to a station and showed me how to pack freshly polished mortar projectiles into crates with Wehrmacht stenciling. There was a quota I had to meet lest I be punished. Presumably the other women on the line would also be punished for my lack of diligence. The machinery caused a din and heat and the factory air stank of oil and sweat which seeped into your uniform and skin.

The woman before me died last week.

Lunchtime. We were marched back to the mess hall for more than soup and a smaller morsels of bread. I was hungry this time and consumed every drop and crumb. Back to the factory and the mortar crates. By mid-afternoon I was exhausted and achy but kept at it until early evening. Another trek to the mess hall for soup, potato, and tea. The *Aufseherin* met me there and escorted me back to the medical building where I was issued a towel and soap and led to a shower. It was quite welcome. The water was warm and it didn't turn cold during my five minutes. Back in my quarters I was given a fresh uniform and a pair of men's briefs. The *Aufseherin* apologized most insincerely. They were oversized but clean. She instructed me to rinse out the dress I wore that day in the basin and hang it near the window.

It was near dark and whistles blew ordering the inmates inside their barracks which were then locked from the outside by a wooden plank into iron slots. Guard towers and barbed wire could be seen in the twilight and later when a searchlight stabbed across the gloom.

Morning came too soon and another day at the mess hall, assembly yard, and ammunition factory followed. Again and again, day after day. I came to recognize the screams I heard the first night and I imagined what they looked like and how they were called and what their lives had once been like.

I fell into a soul-numbing routine and began to think Reinhard had either lied to me about a temporary stay or had been overruled by Berlin. I was a Buchenwald inmate.

After a month I was gaunt and dispirited. I expected my hair to be shorn any day. Nonetheless, I had separate quarters and a woman inmate and *Aufseherin* assigned to me.

LIFE AND DEATH IN BUCHENWALD

Another morning came with shouts and groans and screams. The *Aufseherin* escorted me to the dining hall. Along the way there was a horse-drawn wagon hauling a half dozen or so corpses.

"Many die in the night. The bodies are placed outside the blocks and a work detail gathers them and takes them to a burn pit after roll call. The corpses have to be entered into the books. Some must have died a few days ago judging by the stench. Hurry!"

The late fall of 1943 became early winter and we inmates took in formation while roll call took place. Sometimes there was drizzle or sleet or snow that soaked the work dresses. The officers took their time, waiting several minutes to handle statistics that only required a few seconds to enter into the books.

"They want us to drop and die in the cold," a woman said.

"The next selection will be terrible," said another as he breathed deeply.

"Another train is coming in," said a third.

An SS woman overheard talk and struck one of the women with a baton. She fell to the ground and the beating continued despite the cries.

"Eyes to the front!" came the command from the officer of the day. "Eyes to the front at all times!"

We proceeded to the arms factory. On the way we passed a

makeshift gallows where three corpses were dangling in the cold wind. They remained there for several days. There were other ways to instill fear. Some who violated an even minor transgression, or who were chosen for no reason, were ordered to stand at attention for hours on end. If they faltered they were beaten. When they fell they were shot. I imagined that they seen their last few hours thinking of loved ones, hoping for justice someday, then leaning over.

I tried to get an idea of what lay ahead for me. How much longer was my sentence? Would I ever leave? Would I meet my end at the assembly yard or get packed into a train bound for Poland? I used all my powers to get answers. The only image I saw was a very dim light in the distance. I took that as a good sign.

Most of the women wanted nothing to do with me. They smiled faintly and nodded but conversations were few and short and shallow. Most saw me led to and from my quarters by a guard and knew that something was up. There were whispers. "She's an informer" and "She's one of the officers' whores". One girl, maybe seventeen, spoke with me every now and then. I knew her from the mess hall my first day when she said we had to hurry to make roll call. We worked at the same plant, not far apart. Her face was as grim as the rest but with glimmers of youthful sweetness that did not last long.

Amid the din of the shop floor I noticed an SS guard speak briefly with the plant's chief *Aufseherin*, who nodded. He walked down the floor as women looked straight down at their work and stopped at my youthful friend. With an air of resignation she accompanied him to a back area. Twenty minutes later he walked back down the floor and left. The young woman, fighting back tears, returned to her station shortly later. The other women sent consoling glances her way.

On the way back to the mess hall that day I tried to express sympathy but she cut me off. We all do what we have to do here. I do, they do, and so do you."

"I pray that this will end someday. Someday soon."

"You are naive – and pitiable! Do you really think anyone is listening to prayers? Look around!" She motioned wildly with her arms. "Look around! Look all around us!" She laughed dryly and cynically until an *Aufseherin's* baton came down on her head and got her back in step.

Only a few days later the same guard came to the factory one more and began the same whispered conversation with the *Aufseherin,* who this time seemed perturbed. I cannot be sure why. It might have been she had a sense of responsibility for her girls though it might be more likely that the commandant's office had strict production quotas and the guard's intermittent forced sex with a worker interfered with it. Who would be blamed for a production shortfall, she or a guard?

The man swaggered down the shop floor and everyone knew his destination. He passed girl after girl, sending each a leer as though he might favor them on his next visit until he came upon his victim, the same from a few days earlier. She kept her eyes on her work hoping he would go on but a tap on her head made it clear he would not. He put an arm around her and walked her to the back room. The others focused all the more on their work. Some wept. Machines whirred, assembly lines churned.

The girl came back to the floor with a look of consternation. The *Aufseherin* ran to her, then sent one of the girls for help. An officer and guard arrived, went to the backroom, and after half an hour carried out the lifeless form of the rapacious guard. A lively conversation between the officer and the *Aufseherin* was lost amid the noise of the shop floor but in time the body was removed and the girl was led away. Random visits and interruptions by guards fell sharply.

BECK ARRIVES

One evening there was a knock. The *Aufseherin* was never so formal.

"Bertha? Bertha Siegelman?"

The tentative voice was that of Reinhard Beck. I was undoubtedly the first Jew to be pleased to have an SS officer at her door. In fact I wanted to embrace him.

"Bertha, I hope you are well. I brought you chicken from the officers mess. I trust you will find it more to your liking than camp food. Has anyone laid hands on you?"

"No. I have seen beatings but none has come my way."

"I shall see it continues to be the case."

"Has anything about my situation here changed?"

"I don't think so. Berlin wants to frighten you, break you, make you grateful for the previous arrangement, and eager to do your work for them. The orders were to put you in one of the women's blocks and have you subjected to all the cruelties the rest must endure. It takes a toll."

"So, you saw to it that I received special treatment?"

"Yes. Who else?"

"No one. No one at all. Not in here, not in Munich."

"I care about you, Bertha. I care very much about you. You know that. What I've done wasn't easy and it isn't without risks. I want you to get through this and I want us to get through the war. I have no control over that, however. There are millions of people around the world trying desperately to kill other people. We are just two people."

"Two people with wiles."

We embraced warmly and enduringly. Too enduringly. A throat cleared in the doorway and there stood Hanke, the SS officer I saw the first day and only occasionally since. Just behind him was the *Aufseherin* with a smug look.

"Sturmbannführer Beck, how good of you to visit my camp. In the future, however, you will check in at the administration building with me personally or my assistant. Camp rules. And there is another camp rule that I must underscore for you. There will be no personal relationships between personnel and prisoners. There is also a very strict regulation against relationships between SS soldiers and Jews. You may have Berlin's ear on many matters, that is well known throughout the SS, but if word got out of this sordid display your reputation would be tarnished and penalties would be imposed."

The two men were the same rank, the equivalent of majors in most armies, but authority is a nuanced matter and men are ever in competition with one another for power. Hanke had just promoted himself over Reinhard.

"Though I of course appreciate your concern with appearances I do not need instructions on rules. Not those involving officers and prisoners, nor those involving officers and *Aufseherinen*."

Reinhard just demoted him.

"And your concern with rules will be noted in my reports. Now, please proceed to the administration building and sign in, as required."

"I shall, of course. But first I have to share some communications between Berlin and your special guest. That will be all, Hanke."

Reinhard glared menacingly and nodded his head. Hanke stewed but complied, as did his *Aufseherin*.

"Reinhard! I read those two the same way. You indeed missed your calling."

"Bertha, any man could see what was going on there. Hanke is notorious. Koch gives him wide latitude here and he exercises it. He shoots people for sport, rapes women inmates, and wastes no opportunity to elevate his power and weaken that of others."

"Except for Koch's power."

"And Koch's wife. She resides here and uses her indirect authority to engage in orgies and torture people. We must not run afoul of those three."

"Reinhard, just what is your position in the SS?" I whispered.

"Officially, I work with army counterintelligence as an observer, a problem solver. Berlin entrusts me to keep tabs on people who might be merely inefficient and incompetent and then there are people who might be embarrassing or disloyal."

"Then the SS must be wary of you."

"Mostly, yes. But the Wehrmacht is under my purview as well. The old-line Prussians mostly loathed Hitler but they were cashiered and replaced by loyalists like Keitel and Jodl."

"So the army is loyal now."

"There is grumbling, especially after the debacles in Russia."

"And you inform on them?"

"Not since the debacles in Russia. But more on this another time. Until then let us both be on guard and I will get you out of this place as soon as I can."

"This Hanke fellow. I have thoughts he has a powerful benefactor. A relative perhaps."

"His uncle is a general in the Waffen SS – Sepp Dietrich. He's deeply loyal to Hitler and it is reciprocated. Dietrich commands a corps. Several divisions, tens of thousands of men and many panzers."

"In France."

"Correct."

Some days are so disturbing that you know your sleep will be fitful and plagued by dreadful images.

Fires and smoke in the east were coming closer. More and more trains filled with emaciated prisoners and mutilated soldiers. Generals and prostitutes cavorted in elegant dining cars, oblivious to the other passengers. A man was trying to get into engineer's compartment. He had an eye patch and was different from the others. Reinhard watched him and did not try to stop him.

HANKE

I lay on my cot listening to inmates chatting outside their blocks before lights out. It was refreshing and inspiring to hear a little laughter. In the distance Russian men sang something that sounded like a folk song in deep voices.

The door opened and there stood Hanke, leaning cockily against the jamb. I suddenly thought of the corpses on the gallows.

"Guten Abend, Frau Bertha. I hope you are adjusting well to your work surroundings and I trust it has been impressed upon you that your labor is essential to Germany whether it is in a factory or a darkened parlor – with crystal ball or a deck of cards."

"Everything is just how I envisioned it."

"Good to hear! And that brings me to the purpose of my visit. It is my understanding that you have demonstrated an uncanny ability to foresee events in the war. We are at a critical point. Britain and the United States are poised to strike in the West. They will land in France. That is clear. But where in France? What do you see?"

"Just as you operate best in a certain environment, I do my work best in comfortable surroundings."

"You must realize that you are one of the most comfortable people in all Buchenwald. Just ask the women you work with. Ask those Russian men bleating out there. Have you heard of the building here called the 'doll house'? In other camps such places are called the 'joy section'. They are brothels! Houses of whores!"

"That is where you and the officers and guards display your manliness, I suppose."

"Wrong, Jew witch! We have other places for that. The brothel is for the inmates. If they show the proper spirit in their labor they are rewarded with a token that buys them an hour of delirious pleasure. It was Himmler's idea. Ingenious fellow! I can place you in the camp brothel within the hour!"

"No, thank you. I have a better idea for my accommodations. A cot in a bare room in a prison camp does not rise to the level of comfortable surroundings and I must insist on returning home, where of course I can serve your Reich to my fullest. That is important to you and your superiors. I might even be able to tell you the date and place of the invasion in France. That will enable your panzer forces to be positioned to respond." That struck something inside him. "Yes, yes, the panzer forces will be of great importance in the year 1944. That is of more than purely military importance to you, is it not. Ah wait! You have a brother there."

"No!"

"Another relative then. Perhaps a cousin. Ahh, it's an uncle! Why did I to see that immediately. The preparations are meticulous, the soldiers trained and motivated, the leadership carefully chosen. Ah, but I can see no more. Not here. Not in this wretched place. Herr Hanke, I will be so much more helpful in my own element. Home. Home in Munich. The Führer visited me there. We spoke at length there and he benefited from my counsel."

"I shall convey your request to the commandant and to higher echelons. I may also have to convey your coziness with another SS officer."

He leered at me and came over to my cot. Sexual and violent urges are closely fused in many men. Too many, really. Hanke lurched from the former to the latter in an instant and slapped me.

"Jew witch! What spells are you casting? You presume to barter with me? I am an officer! I give orders! Do you see those men hanging in the assembly yard? They are there because it is my will that they are there!"

His blows fell hard and fast commingled with sexual arousal. He tore away my nightgown and quickly opened his tunic and dropped his trousers. I screamed but nobody would respond to a common enough matter. There was nothing more I could do but avoid further beatings and put my mind somewhere else while I endured what the other women of Buchenwald endured, whether in factory backrooms or sheds or in the bordello, until his eyes lost their ferocity and he went limp.

His hatred and lust expended for the night, he stared intently at me. He had had his conquest but what other plans did he have. I thought he might kill me right then and have some poor inmates hurl my lifeless form onto a horse-drawn cart. He composed himself and put his uniform back on.

"Not a word of this, *klar*!"

"One more thing, *darling*. I will need maps of France and newspapers as well – to better serve Germany, of course. That is why you came here, is it not."

The *Aufseherin* came to my room at the usual hour. She brought maps and newspapers.

STELLA

There was quite a commotion in my quarters one evening shortly after work. A doctor and a few nurses spoke cautiously not far from my door and paced back and forth. The same thing happened the following evening. Something was going on but I could not sense what it was. The next morning, shortly after daybreak, I saw a young woman, an inmate in her teens, spirited inside by a pair of nurses and Stella, the young woman who occasionally brought me meals. That evening I asked her what was going on but she was too fearful to say.

I heard whispers at the mess hall and in formation as we marched to and from the plant. A girl at another shop is pregnant. Everyone knew that such women were put on the next train for Poland where she and her unborn child would be put to death immediately. From what we had heard listening in on guards the method was poison gas in specially-constructed buildings. The idea of a young woman and her child being killed in such a horrible way struck us all, hardened though we were from beatings and killings and rapes and the sight of rotting corpses hanging from gallows.

Stella came in one evening and I offered her some sausage and eggs and said she could take some back with her. I asked her where she was from, though her accent told the tale.

"I was born in Tübingen and grew up there. My parents owned a dress shop and were involved with the Socialist Party. The Gestapo came for us in 1938 and sent us here."

"What of your parents?"

141

"Ohh…We were separated upon arrival. I ask people at the mess hall and outside the blocks before lights out. One woman said my mother was working at a sub-camp near the old Austrian border. As for my father, well, there's no word. None. I ask the men when I pass them and I can see they want to help me but they only shake their heads sadly. I can only pray my parents are well."

"I hope they are, too. Do you know why I am here, Stella?" She averted her eyes and looked uncomfortable. "I am not the mistress of the commandant or anyone else. I am no one's woman but my own since those bastards out there killed my father, probably not from where we are sitting this very moment. Nor am I an informer or spy or rat."

"I can see in your eyes that you have a fierce independent spirit."

"I see it in you as well, Stella. That's the key to surviving here. Otherwise you sink into despair."

"And then you fail a selection and you are on the train to hell."

"I am here because I am a seer and certain well-placed people respect my gift. I use it against them though they do not know it yet. Perhaps they will someday."

Her eyes widened. "Then they will deal very harshly with you!"

"Yes. They will reserve a seat for me on the next train to hell."

"A seat? Ha!"

She covered her mouth as she giggled sweetly and quietly.

"Stella, who is the young woman being hidden here? I have heard she is with child."

"She was raped repeatedly by a number of guards. That is the fate of most young women here."

Stella has been taken to a shed behind the medical buildings.

"She kept working though her monthly flows had stopped but she was beginning to show even underneath the work dress. One of the girls told a doctor here of her plight and he came up with a plan to hide her near the typhus ward and put her on the manifest as one of those testing vaccines."

"Is he going to perform an abortion?"

"He offered to do just that but the girl is resisting that. She and her baby will either live or die together."

"I see, I see. The typhus ward is not an ideal place but it is the most isolated location in all Buchenwald."

"No one goes there who does not have to. So she is off the manifest for work details and treated well in here. Better food, a nice cot, and no hard labor or groping guards."

"The doctor is very brave and honorable. Is he SS?"

"Of course not. Dr Ackerknecht is an inmate because of his political opposition to the Nazis. His skills are being used by the camp. The commandant knows how to get the most from us. There are jewelers who inspect confiscated rings and watches before they are distributed to officers or sold in Munich. There are engineers who draw up blueprints for new buildings and nurses who work here and in the infirmary. The doctor helps us where he can. He sees we are treated as best he can. He minimizes the suffering. When someone is in great pain and has no chance he...well, he sees that the suffering does not take a long time."

Hypodermic needle...understanding faces... sleep.

"What of the baby? What will happen when birth comes?"

"That is six months away. We are trying to find a civilian worker here who will take the newborn out and pace it in a convent. Dr Ackerknecht has a few promising persons. We have hope. We have to have hope. Otherwise we lose our minds and die."

Whistles blew and inmates trudged back to the dank, overcrowded blocks for the night. Searchlights darted across the mud and sky. A single rifle shot sounded a few hundred meters away.

"Before you leave, Stella, a question that has been nagging me for quite some time. What happens to all the corpses here? Are they buried outside the perimeter?"

"On the far side of camp there is a crematory. From the mess hall you can see the tall chimney in the distance. You must notice the soot on the windows. Some of it is from coal plants, some is from the far side of Buchenwald."

We wept and held each other as long as we dared. I looked into her with all my will and saw only darkness. I kissed her forehead as she got up to leave and hoped to see her again.

The *Aufseherin* escorted me to the mess hall the following morning.

"The SS officer who brought me here a few months ago told me there is typhus research going on here. At first I thought he should not have mentioned it but people in the *Abwehr* know what they can and cannot divulge. So what of this typhus matter?"

"I know of you and your contacts. That's why you are with me and not in a stinking block. Our brave men are exposed to typhus in southern Russia and we are doing our part to see they are protected from it. A vaccine is being developed that will be a major contribution to medicine and help the war effort tremendously. If it weren't for contagious diseases our men would be in Moscow this day."

"I see. So the disease is a serious problem. I only wish there were something I could do to help the research."

"You are a Jew."

"Yes, but typhus does not look at anyone's religion. It hits everyone it can and as hard as it can. I hope the vaccine saves lives. It is wonderful to know that amazing things are going on in the building I find myself in."

"Be quiet and go eat. You have your work at the factory."

I looked to the distance and saw the tall chimney spewing smoke into the Thuringian sky.

Just before lights out Stella tapped on my door and I bade her to come in.

"Bertha, this is Sarah. She is the one I told you about who has recently become part of Dr Ackerknecht's typhus experiments."

"Come in, young ladies, and make yourself comfortable in my plush dwelling. I would serve you wine and hors d'oeuvres but alas my servant is off this evening. However, I have some rye from the officers mess."

It was refreshing to hear them giggle like the young women they were. Sarah sat next to me and Stella rested against a wall. Clearly, they were here for my thoughts.

"We know things," Stella said." We overhear things. The nurses let things out after a while. They do so in whispers and to people they trust and care for."

"There is something out of the ordinary about the typhus program?" I asked.

"Yes, there is. Something out of the ordinary in a terribly daring way. The trials have found a successful vaccine that Commandant Koch is boasting about to Berlin. It's supposed to be distributed to German troops across Europe and save countless lives and help win the war."

"But that will not happen," Sarah added. "The vaccine will not save any soldiers' lives."

My gift was not helping but my cynicism commingling with hope were compensating admirably.

"So, there's no vaccine – no, there *is* a vaccine but a substitute with no medicinal value will be sent to the troops – a saline solution. Millions of little bottles of salt water."

"For the most part yes, but some vaccines will be sent out so that there is some evidence the vaccine is working," said Stella.

"Oh yes. Terribly daring – and a contribution to the war effort though a negative one. I see, I see. Why are you telling me this? Ahh, you want something from me."

Stella and Sarah fell silent and knelt at my feet and lay their shaved heads on my lap. They whimpered and wept for several minutes.

"We want to know. We want to know if we will live through this."

"I want to know what will happen to my baby. Please."

I leaned down and pressed their heads to my breast and immersed myself into the sea as never before. Fires, fires, and more fires on a dark foreboding horizon.

"In the distance I see lights. Three lights merging as one."

They wept all the more and hugged me, then as whistles blew, they headed to the corridor leading to their cots. I lay back on mine and cried for hours.

No more than a week later Hanke discovered that a pregnant woman was being hidden in the typhus research ward. He and a guard stormed into the room and dragged poor Sarah outside and hurled her to her knees. Hanke drew his pistol and before she could scream, fired a shot into her forehead. Stella witnessed the murder from a window.

But as the words over the main gate said, everyone gets what they deserve. Not long thereafter Hanke became quite ill and was sent to the infirmary where it was suspected he had typhus. Fortunately, the camp had an expert on the subject and so Dr Ackerknecht was summoned. The good doctor of course applied all his skills and knowledge but Hanke's condition weakened every day. His fever stayed unbearably high and he lost a considerable amount of weight. Dr Ackerknecht had Stella brought in from the typhus ward to help by applying cold compresses. They were neither caringly nor regularly applied despite Hanke's worsening conditions and increasingly feeble pleas.

As his breathing and pulse indicated the end was near she leaned to his ear and whispered, "The Jew witch said the Reich will lose the war and your kind will be hanged."

There was a brief look of horror, then nothing.

REUNION

ope that Hanke would use his clout to get me back to Munich ended with his death. He richly deserved death though a measure of justice beforehand would have been preferable. As it was, he was gone and another would soon replace him. There were no shortages of Hankes and Kochs. One did take his place but he did not favor me with a visit and he probably knew nothing of my gift. He probably only knew that I was hands off and that his predecessor had stepped into the typhus building once too often.

The drudgery continued. The *Aufseherin* marched me to the mess hall, then it was off to roll call and the factory. After work Stella usually brought a good meal from the officers mess which I shared with her while we listened to voices chatting and singing in the distance before lights out. Life went on. Somehow, improbably, life went on.

I had heard nothing from Reinhard in weeks. He might have been killed in an air raid or run afoul of Berlin and executed. I sensed he was still alive though.

A lovely spring morning seemed to offer good things but the mess hall food put a damper on expectations. Windows and doors were open to allow ventilation into an otherwise fetid, malodorous chamber packed with a hundred or so women for whom hygiene was a fading memory.

I sat off to one side, hardly by myself but the other still considered me with suspicion even though they saw me there with Stella every now and then. Someone sat beside me, clutched my arm, and whispered with restrained elation.

"Bertha! Bertha, my child! Please make no show of surprise or affection. They may use it against us."

It was my mother! She was alive! Her face was gaunt and her eyes sunken back into her head but she had survived for all those months! We leaned against each other and held hands and spoke as we wept.

"Oh mother, I feared the worst! I truly did. You are alive and right beside me!"

"As it was intended, my child."

"Where is you work?"

"They sent me here from a sub-camp last week I sew uniforms in a building not far from your arms plant. I saw you marched there a few mornings ago. My health is all things considered good though. Seeing you is an elixir!"

"I have not felt more alive in a year! They sent me here as punishment. For how long I cannot say. But I have power. I have influence. I am trying to get out of here and I will get you out as well."

"Ohhhh! How wonderful that would be. Home! Home!"

"Is father still alive? I heard —"

"They took him away during roll call a long time ago. He looked back to get a last glimpse of me. He disappeared behind a building and there was a burst of fire." She wiped tears.

The chimney in the distance.

"Raus! Raus!" came the angry shouts of the *Aufseherinen* and we had to head out for roll call.

We scurried out to the assembly yard. I was happy for the first time in months and enjoyed the classical music over the loudspeakers.

Stella said there was no way to bring my mother to the medical building and no guard would look the other way. There was something to look forward to at the morning meal now, breakfast with mother again, though in an environment completely unlike home. As much as I wanted to race to the mess hall I knew that would suggest to the

Aufseherin that something was afoot and she might come in to find out just what. So mother and I met at the side and held hands under the table while we ate. Just being together was glorious and as much as wanted to talk we had to take in nourishment for the day ahead.

"Is your health holding up, mother?"

"Yes. I have had bouts with chest colds and when they come we always wonder if tuberculosis or another dread disease has struck me. They have peculiar ways of treating the sick here."

"They do indeed. Good spirits and making the most out of what little we have to eat are all we have."

"Who are these powerful men you know, young lady?"

"Oh, there is only one and his name is not important."

"I hope he can help. And Bertha, if you can find a way out, go! By all means go! Do not delay a single day for me! Do you hear me? We can both live through this! Both of us!"

"Raus! Raus!"

A knock came that evening and I knew who it was.

"Reinhard!" I rushed into his arms the instant the door closed, much to my surprise. And his as well.

We held each other closely and lovingly. Caresses came naturally enough, then soft kisses, but nothing further.

"Hanke is dead, you know. Typhus."

"News reached me in Munich. A new man will be sent soon enough."

"He's already here. Could he be worse than Hanke?"

"Oh yes. Hanke was starchy and arrogant and had a sadistic streak but there are worse. Some are so vicious that quotas suffer and Berlin takes note. Others cause junior officers and enlisted men to volunteer for combat duty just to get away or because they want to die. Mauthausen and Treblinka are bad. Auschwitz is the most notorious. It has killed several million people to this day."

"What!"

"At first I thought the numbers were idle boasts from zealous camp commandants trying to curry favor in Berlin. Inspectors are sent and they return with what they see as splendid news of a policy put into practice by devoted functionaries."

"The trains from here with the sick and exhausted go to Auschwitz?"

"Or one of the other death camps in Poland. There are four. They operate night and day."

"There are that many people sent there?"

"People are rounded up all across Europe, packed into trains, and sent to their deaths. It goes on and on. I know of no more details. May we shift to the purpose of my visit? I mean I wanted to come see you, very much so. I feel human again. I hope my embrace told you that."

"Yes, Reinhard, it did. In a wonderful way. This place does not ordinarily offer a suitable environment for affection. Now, to the purpose of your visit."

"I have convinced the higher-ups that you have learned from your time here and will perform your services well and make no more efforts to escape."

I recognized where this was going and the dilemma it posed.

"Your gift is needed more than ever now that the allies are poised to invade France. Rome is about to fall and the Red Army cannot be stopped no matter which field marshal Berlin entrusts the job to. I've convinced Berlin to return you to your home tomorrow."

"I cannot!"

"What! What do you mean you cannot? You see what goes on here! You see how precarious life is here!"

"My mother is here. I saw her in the mess hall last week. I cannot leave without her. We will have to bring her along tomorrow."

"That, my dear, is utterly out of the question. Do you know what I went through to get permission for you?"

"Reinhard, did you know my mother was alive?"

"I knew it was possible. After your father was executed your mother disappeared into the sub-camp system. People come and go there. My inquiries led nowhere. People live and die there. Your mother was not young and I did not want to give you false hope."

"I want her out."

"I want her out too but I cannot simply drive out the gate with two passengers, at least not now. I do not know your mother but I know mothers and yours would want you to leave. Has she told you that?"

"She has. Whenever I see her."

"Then we leave tomorrow."

"After the morning in the mess hall."

The *Aufseherin* arrived and had been briefed on my departure.

"I will take breakfast in the mess hall, however I will not be attending roll call or work today."

Eyebrows raised and off we went. I found mother at the side table and sat down next to her with my breakfast.

"Good morning, mother."

"Good morning, dear."

"Mother, I have the opportunity to leave today."

"Wonderful! I am very happy."

"But you, mother."

"You are leaving today. That's all there is to it. Your mother insists – and your mother is very happy!"

"I know, I know. We will get you out. It will take time but we will get you out."

"I know you will. But for now, you get out of here this very day and get back your health. You must not be eating well!"

"Oh, mother! No humor now. You must eat and take my portions as well. You have a day's work ahead of you."

"And you have a long life ahead of you."

"Raus! Raus!"

We washed our bowls and utensils and mother headed for the assembly yard with all the others. I left my bowl at the basin and left for my quarters where Reinhard would meet me in an hour. Mother looked back at me as she took her place and smiled. No one felt a mother's love more than I did at that moment.

Reinhard was on time. I had little to take along expect for the maps of France, which I had all but memorized anyway. I said goodbye to Stella and wished her the best as we embraced, we drove past long lines of weary inmates and rows of dreary brick factories, then out the main gate of Buchenwald.

MUNICH

The journey back south was unpleasant on many counts. I could not shake the feeling that I was abandoning the woman who gave me life even though I was obeying her wish – no, her order. I was also leaving Stella behind and the scores of women and girls I worked and ate with and untold thousands of others who were living in squalor and despair and terror. And here I was being driven home by an SS officer.

More damaged cities. Off in the distance were smoldering ruins and people trudging down the roads in search of places to live. Military convoys were everywhere of course. The vehicles looked older and lacked the energy of a few years earlier.

"Has Berlin been bombed?"

"Very heavily. The British at night, the Americans by day. Whole districts have been reduced to rubble. Many civilians are dead. They come every day and every night to one city or another. More and more they use incendiary bombs rather than high explosives."

We came to a village and entered a tavern. The walls had pictures of local boys in the service. Some had a black ribbon fixed on the side.

Interment...freshly dug earth...grieving faces.

They were proud to have an SS officer as a guest and asked him when the secret weapons would be used to turn the tide. Reinhard told them that Berlin was biding its time.

I thought of the newsreel footage from the Nuremberg rally and all the wide-eyed faces and ecstatic cheering. There were still many faithful followers, perhaps especially in rural areas where blood and soil shape life and the bombs and rubble are far away.

We arrived at Munich in the early evening. My district had been spared. A guard detail was waiting at the door. Lauman was not among them. Reinhard gave me my key and said he would come by in the morning. I raced up the stairs and swung the door open to my home. It was dusty and musty but in good order. There were plates and glasses on the table so someone had been using the place for one thing or another. I changed the bed linens and lay down. I looked to the side where Joshua once slept, kissed the pillow, and somehow fell asleep in a few moments.

I was awakened by sirens and not thirty minutes later the droning sounds came from above and loud explosions came from downtown. It was not a dream like the ones of the east and Stalingrad. The explosions continued and at times became frighteningly thunderous, so much so that the building tumbled and windows are close to shattering. Outside the window was a redness from flames only two or three kilometers away, fiercely accented by occasional bright flashes. Hellish winds sounded like immense trains speeding by at great speed. Trees were uprooted, trucks tumbled wildly. Shouts and screams were everywhere.

The raid eased but not for long. More planes, hundreds of them, came overhead and antiaircraft guns in the suburbs sent up a storm of explosive shells, fragments of which hit the streets and roofs near me. The rumbling began anew and the flames erupted, this time in another part of Munich.

The sun rose, albeit reluctantly and with difficulty as so much smoke had to be overcome. A third raid came in the late morning. The bombs fell about ten kilometers away. Only by mid-afternoon did it end.

I looked out on the street and saw the guards had taken shelter somewhere. I stayed upstairs even though I had no food. Munich was still ablaze.

The next day the guard detail returned and two of them escorted me to the marketplace where my gracious benefactors had established a line of credit for me. The faces were ashen and frightened. The talk was that the old city had been leveled. Not a building was left. Telephone lines were down and the buses weren't running.

I stocked up with what little was there and returned home. I expected to see signs of fatigue and doubt in the guards but there was none. True believers. True believers far from the fronts. I ate and read an unabridged copy of Gibbon's study of the Roman Empire that I purchased in graduate school. I hoped to finish it as Berlin fell.

Reinhard visited a day or so later and took me to the park. More grim faces and a dozen or so young men with amputated limbs. Many people were in a daze, staring ahead blankly and mumbling. Loved ones saw to them and encouraged them to feed pigeons and take part in conversation.

"What of my mother, Reinhard? Is she well? Can you get her out of that place?" Even though Munich was no longer safe I wanted her out of Buchenwald.

"I don't know with any certainty, Bertha. I am busy with work. The hour is at hand in France. I hope to spirit her out and get her to a safe place outside the city, the home of a trusted person. I am doing what I can. Believe me."

My father. He knows more about my father.

"Reinhard, did you see my father die?"

"I did not. I am aware he was executed but I have no more information than that."

"Yes, you do."

"Ah, your gift tells you so."

"It does, and your nervousness tells me too."

"Well, we have to make difficult decisions – terrible decisions, ones we do not wish to discuss."

"Some decisions must be discussed if we are friends and honorable."

"Ach... This is difficult."

"Everything today is difficult. Go on."

"After your last escape attempt I was told to impress upon you that patience was running out. It was to be made perfectly clear to you that you were angering higher-ups and the best way to do that was to kill your parents. I said one parent only but that was insufficient."

"You ordered my father to be killed but you spared mother. You spared her in a certain way. You had her disappear into the sea of inmates at Buchenwald."

"Yes, that is correct. She would be off the books and have a chance of surviving."

"Just like any other inmate. Did you know she was alive when I arrived there?"

"I did not. I only knew she had been sent to a sub-camp where she would work indoors. I am pleased she is well, all things considered. And I will do my best to get her out. That I promise you. Now, let us turn to what lies ahead for you. As I said, the hour is at hand in France and you will have callers, probably generals. The most logical of military minds are looking high and low for a way to determine where the allies will land. The timing is fairly well known – early June. The vexing thing is precisely where. Most think the Pas de Calais. Others think just to the west in Normandy."

"And where do you think it will be? You are in counterintelligence. You must have your ears open."

"Indeed I do. My ears have listened to many people and heard many briefings. I only know that the consensus says the Pas de Calais. That is where the panzer divisions are concentrated for counterattack, including Sepp Dietrich's corps. There are several dissenters who think it will be Normandy and one of them is very important."

"Who is this very important person? Would I know his name?"

"Oh yes. I believe you have made his acquaintance in your parlor."

"Hitler believes the attack will come at Normandy? Then why are the panzers concentrated elsewhere?"

"He is deferring to the generals on the matter. He is not the same man after Stalingrad and Stalin's steady advances on Berlin."

"Does he feel remorse?"

"I doubt he's capable of it. I suspect he feels a noose being placed around his neck."

"One can hope."

"And one can prepare. You will be visited soon. Wehrmacht generals."

"I must prepare. The hour as you say is at hand."

"If you would be so kind as to take a look inside a briefcase someone carelessly left in your parlor you will find interesting reading material."

"How thoughtful of someone."

OVERLORD AND
VALKYRIE I

T he black leather briefcase lay where he said it would. I pulled
a worn strap from the buckle enclosure and opened it wide,
revealing hundreds of pages of documents and photographs.
They were marked "OKH" and "OB West" and had the smell of
ink from a duplicating machine. Leafing through the documents
told me that "OKH" was army high command, "OB West" was
the headquarters in Paris and the reports were on German troops
positions in northern France, allied troop locations and embarkation
ports, likely invasion locations, and response plans.

At the back of the pile were aerial photographs of allied docks,
ships, commanding generals and their biographies, and ground
images of German bunkers and obstacles along French beaches. One
photograph showed a German general in a heavy overcoat standing
on a fortified position while a young soldier manned a machine gun.
I poured through the documents like a student preparing for an exam
in a subject she did not want to study but she had an exam for. Two
or three days past. I was noticing different writing styles and the
occasional typo. Shame, shame.

It was clear that there was a strong consensus that the allies
would land in the Pas de Calais. Study after study noted it was
the shortest distance from England and offered a direct path to
Germany's industrial region and Berlin.

As much as I used my gift to discern the invasion spot I could not.

I only saw images of thousands of ships, stormy waters, gray skies, and murderous battle along sandy stretches. I could not, then, tell my next visitors the right or wrong invasion site. There was another way to cause dismay, though it had risks.

Reinhard sent a message by courier – my telephone had been disconnected and not yet returned to working order – that two men would arrive the following morning and suggested there be no reading material lying around. I put the pile of documents into the wood-burning oven and set them alight. They crinkled and writhed and turned into negatives as the spreading flames consumed them and sent them into the skies over the city.

Ten o'clock and a car arrived. Two men in civilian attire climbed the stairs and I met them at the doorway and showed them to the darkened parlor. We sat and I read them. It was not difficult. Though not in uniform, these were military men – and in every sense of the word. They were stiff and orderly but without the aristocratic airs of the Junker caste. Nor were they SS as those people had decided lower-class mannerisms and accents.

When they spoke to exchange introductions, which did not include their names, it was clear they were raised in southern Germany, probably Wurtemberg. One wore spectacles and did most of the talking though I sensed the other was his superior. I further sensed they were men of keen rationality and logic and not well-disposed to my trade. Yet they were here. I also felt diminishing faith in the Reich. They were once faithful German officers but no longer. I sensed more and wanted to know more.

"Frau Siegelman," the bespectacled man said, "you are highly recommended. Your psychic abilities are said to be unrivaled and thought to have helped guide Germany through this war. We have studied the invasion in great detail and consulted with scores of military and logistical experts."

I closed my eyes as though in deep thought and whispered, "Are you OKH or OB West?"

The men exhibited no response but there was no mistaking a pause. They had worked together for many years.

"Those are the names of army headquarters that do not concern us at the moment," said the other man. "We seek to take in, well, unconventional opinions as well. Your thoughts on coming events in France. You were apprised of our visit and undoubtedly have given the matter some thought."

I again closed my eyes for effect.

"I see thousands of brave men...storm-tossed ships...high fortresses...and a vast, bloody struggle for control of sand and soil. In the north, near Dieppe or to the west near Caen. I cannot see with more detail...I see deceit by generals...."

This dismayed them. The less talkative one shifted in his chair. He began to look familiar. I continued.

"The American and British generals are engineering a feint. They will strike one place and deliver a second, more important blow at a different place. Beware deceitful generals, no matter what they say or what colors they fly. One must never overreact. That is what the deceivers want."

They remained silent and I believe they were impressed by the talk of deceit, though it initially worried them because they thought I was referring to them, not their allied counterparts. But why? Oh, I felt intrigue in their minds.

The superior glanced over to the bespectacled man and they stood to leave.

"Danke schön, Frau Siegelman. You have been most helpful." He reached into his briefcase and placed a bottle on the table. "I hope you enjoy apple brandy."

"I do. I would invite you both to raise a glass with me but I'm sure you have pressing matters on this day."

"Indeed we do."

They nodded and headed back to their car. Calvados. They left me a bottle of Calvados. A product of Normandy as I recall.

These two men had something absorbing their minds beside

the impending invasion. Not a sweetheart or a horse race either. Something immense involving many others. Something that struck me as both criminal and wonderful. I poured a glass of the brandy and tried to see what was afoot.

Meetings in secret places...fear of betrayal...fear of Hitler and the SS. Death...many deaths. The man in the photograph near the beach fortification...he was just here.

CALVADOS IN THE NIGHT

I n the middle of May 1944 Reinhard came by. We hugged warmly at the doorway, in part because he was my sole human contact now, in part because I was beginning to love him. I knew he loved me.

"Come, let us sit in the parlor and enjoy a glass of Calvados."

"I do not know what that is but it sounds wonderful."

"A French brandy. Rather strong for me but it has its merits. A pear taste lurks in it."

"I suspect this was a present from recent visitors."

"Correct, Reinhard. They were most appreciative. But first things first."

"Your mother is well and I have placed her in a house to the north of here. The helpers are a Jewish couple who were able to get Christian papers several years ago. There was a great deal of that back then. It keeps the Gestapo busy but I have the file. In fact. That is how I got your mother out. I claimed she knew of such trickery and it was essential to interrogate her – 'for the good of the Reich's security' is how I put it."

"My mother is safe! You clever man! You dear, dear man! I can't thank you enough."

"I interrogated her repeatedly. I asked her if you were as wonderful as a young girl as you are now. She was puzzled."

"Oh, Reinhard! You puzzle me too but in a marvelous way. Mother is in a house in the countryside…near a wooded area."

"I believe so but the details I must keep private. What if the Gestapo gets wind of this and comes for you? Far better that you know no more than you do now."

"And what if they come for you for the same reason?"

"I am prepared for that. I do not know the precise place. Besides, I will take steps to avoid the hospitality of the Gestapo."

A pistol.

"I appreciate your courage and resourcefulness, Reinhard. It may be best that I remain in the dark. Now, I see you are enjoying the brandy my guests so kindly left me. Who were they?"

"Generals in the regular army. I cannot be certain of exactly who they were. I only know that OB West – the command post of forces in France – is very nervous about the allied invasion and Field Marshal von Rundstedt is seeking counsel from all sorts of places."

"And we are presently in one of those places, sipping brandy courtesy of OB West."

"It is not a chateau in Paris but I love it just the same. Better service. Just what did you tell them, or would that be an intrusion on your professional code?!"

"Reinhard, you are well aware that my advice has been to steer the Reich into folly. I was unable to determine where the allies will land so I told them not to commit their backup forces to the invasion because it was a feint, a maneuver intended to fool the German generals into misallocating their troops away from a second invasion site."

"Clever, dear. Quite clever. What if the first invasion site is in fact a trick and the real invasion force will strike elsewhere? That scenario has been run through countless times."

"Either way, I planted the seed of doubt and that may give the allied forces an advantage at the first site, whether it was real or not. They may need it. There are risks but delaying is more likely to cause trouble."

"All the more clever, Bertha. If the invasion site is not the Pas de

Calais, where most think it will be, and there is no second invasion, what then?"

"Then the generals will be all the more likely to keep their backup forces away from the battle."

"Quite right, I hope."

"We have hope. That we have. Reinhard, those men who were here. The generals, that is. I read them quite well but completely. They are involved in something that struck me as both criminal and wonderful. What could that be?"

"I am going to need more of their brandy for that, if I may."

"You may. I see men gathering in rooms decorated in rococo splendor, talking in hushed tones behind drawn curtains. Most are military, others from the old aristocracy. Why would men of such high status be meeting in secret and not in a ministry building in Berlin? The wars have been planned and armies have marched. Why, Reinhard?"

"You have given this great thought, my dear. What is your sense?"

"I think those generals and noblemen want to seize control of the government and possibly to kill Hitler."

"Bertha, there has long been a contingent in the regular army who despised Hitler and wanted him dead. The generals in the 1930s had a plan they called the "clean up" which would oust Hitler and his government. The army had great unity then. It was a compact force limited in size by the Versailles Treaty. The generals were a tight clique. They all knew and trusted one another and their junior officers respected and feared them."

"But nothing happened."

"They delayed. Maybe next year, the timing is not right yet. By 1938 or so the generals no longer had the tight collegiality they once had. It was much larger. The Nazis saw to that when they broke with Versailles."

"Ahh! As the army grew in size the younger officers were pro-Hitler and the generals could no longer be confident that their orders would be obeyed by them," I added.

"Correct. And the SS grew in size and lethality too. The generals did not want a civil war so they waited more and planned in secret. Oh, they have tried to kill Hitler several times over the last few years but the bombs failed to detonate or other generals ordered a halt. Here we are. Germany is on the verge of annihilation."

"I hope these men are successful. Can I help?"

"Probably not. Any word from you could reach Berlin and lead to a swift roundup."

"Reinhard, it sounds as if you're involved!"

"I am not involved in any way. I hear things. I read reports. Counterintelligence is not unaware of ongoing plots."

"Counterintelligence is involved. I feel it."

"Perhaps. Thank you for the brandy, my dear. I must be off."

"Don't go. Please," I found myself saying.

The war I knew was coming to a pivotal point and the Reich would fall next year. As dangerous as the Nazis already were, they would be much more so when defeat neared. They would take as many people down with them as possible, including those poor souls in the camps, anyone remotely suspected of disloyalty, and even a humble fortune teller, regardless if they suspected her of spinning yarns to lead them to defeat. I felt alone and vulnerable.

"My gift tells me you will stay for dinner, Reinhard. I know it with great certainty."

"I do not have your gift but I feel the same way."

And stay he did. I prepared a meal from the meager goods at the grocers and we settled back to enjoy more brandy. I felt that throughout Europe people were seeking comfort and intimacy amid the nightmare. It was so in England, Italy, Hungary, Russia, and Germany. It was no less so in a Munich townhouse that night. Reinhard and I fell into each other's arms and made love through the night, completely, lovingly, and incautiously.

OVERLORD AND VALKYRIE II

In the morning, well past dawn, I awoke again to the sound of air raid sirens and flak. I reached for Reinhard but he was gone. Fortunately, the dread sounds were off in the distance and creeped no closer. I put on a gown and slippers and made my way to the kitchen to make coffee. It had been a while since my benefactors had gotten me real coffee, albeit the rather fierce Turkish variety, so I had to make do with wartime stand-in made from nuts and roots and probably whatever else was lying around. A sudden feeling said the grounds were made in a sub-camp somewhere.

There was a note on the parlor table and I sat down, coffee in hand, to read it. I felt anxiety.

My dearest Bertha,

I am deeply sorry that I made a hasty departure they morning. I wish I could say it was entirely because of duties but that would not be true. Last night as we talked about your father's death I omitted a related matter. I could not bring myself to tell you of it last night and I did not want to look into your eyes this morning and feel compelled to tell you.

Berlin ordered your father's death but also your husband's. It was my task to see that it was followed through by a junior officer. That is one way we have of

166

living with ourselves – ordering others to do things we
do not want to do. So it was by my directive that Joshua
Siegelman was put to death. It was supposed to take place
at Dachau, not your home, not his home, not the home you
two had made for yourselves. The junior officer became
angry and saw fit to kill him before your eyes.

That, however, is not the entire reason for my heavy
heart. I must now confess that putting forward the order
was done with a certain amount of satisfaction. I was in
love with you and I wanted no rival for your affections. I
do not say I could have countermanded the order or found
some way out of it. I say that I am ashamed of the dark
thoughts in my heart as I gave the order.

By way of closing, my dearest Bertha, I must further
confess that I have done worse. I shall of course accept
whatever verdict you feel appropriate for me which I
recognize might be banishing me from your heart forever.

> *With sorrow mixed sweetly with love,*
> *Reinhard*

Our emotions can be quite complex and I was dumbfounded, angry, and touched all at the same instant. I had no idea how I would respond or if I would. The answer never came.

A knock came and a guard brought in a large wooden radio cabinet and plugged it in near the settee in the parlor. I asked who sent it but no one knew. A truck arrived with paperwork. That was all they knew or cared to know. I had an idea, of course. It was most welcome. It allowed me to keep abreast of the news from both Berlin and London and also listen to the Berlin Philharmonic at night as we used to do when there was a semblance of normality in life.

A guard would escort me to the park and the grocer's. Faces were grim and thin. Many young men were maimed and disfigured, their faces hidden by bandages and sunglasses, their loved ones pretending all was well. Gleeful pigeons played in the charade as well.

I drank coffee and nibbled on bread one morning, barely listening to the news. The official broadcast from Berlin, handled by Göbbels's dutiful functionaries, was rather dreary. This and that happened. One city fell to the Russians, then another. All was well though as these were orderly retreats that allowed preparation for a devastating counterattack. The Führer had a plan. Have no fear.

Then after a pause, the announcer, in calm straightforward voice, announced that the allies had begun landings in France that morning. I looked at the calendar – June 6, 1944. The skies were gray and light rain fell outside. The elements I felt were far worse in northern France. The broadcast went to say that the German forces were heroically defending the beaches, spirits were high, generals confident.

"Where is the invasion?" I all but shouted as the announcer went on with confident propaganda. Only after another twenty minutes did he say Normandy.

Turning the dial to the BBC gave me weather reports. Rain in London, speeches in Parliament, the King's visit to a hospital. The only war news was that Rome fell to allied forces the previous day and General Clark was in charge. Nothing on the invasion. Was the German broadcast a deception? Would Berlin boast of driving the allies back across the Channel?

An hour later London reported the invasion was underway and before I could shout for the important detail it confirmed the location – Normandy. So it was on. I went into the sea to attempt to envision the French beaches but could not. My hope of course was that the allies would prevail on the coast, then drive into the heart of the Reich and drive a stake through it, and that hope was so strong it washed away whatever I could envision. It was up to the brave soldiers on the sandy shores.

I looked out the window to the guard detail on the street. They were talking to an officer who was relaying the news. He said this was the opportunity to defeat the British and Americans, then send fresh troops to the east to finish the war on Russia.

That evening one of the guards, knowing I had a radio, tapped at my door and asked for the latest report. I replied there was nothing really new since the late morning and he asked what the BBC was reporting. I saw no ruse in his eyes. He thought London might be more reliable than Berlin. I smiled and said the BBC was saying the same thing as the ministry of information in Berlin. He tipped his cap and turned to leave.

"Oh, young man. Where is the former officer in charge down there. His name was Lauman."

He became solemn and thought if he might be revealing privileged information.

"Frau Siegelman, it is my sad duty to report that our former commander was killed in action while fighting in the east."

My grief was limited. A moment later his face brightened.

"My brother is serving with a panzer division in France this very day! My entire family is proud!"

He tipped his cap again and returned to his post.

I returned to mine at the radio but there were no further developments. A classical performance came on and I listened as I pondered the battles underway and where the reserve divisions were at the moment.

No answer came for several weeks and even then it had to be patched together from news reports, British and German. The reserves were trying put.

On the 20th of July came news, from all sources, that there had been an attempt on the life of Hitler as he conferred with generals on the war in Russia at a command post in East Prussia – the Wolf's Lair as it was known. A bomb had been planted near him, apparently by military officers, but he survived. Alas, the devil lived and his murderousness would continue for the time being. His wrath I felt would be fearsome and it would fall hard upon anyone he suspected of involvement. And of course his suspicion would spread widely and his orders would be executed quickly and remorselessly, even when erroneous.

I had not heard from Reinhard in several weeks and that was

concerning. He knew of plots against Hitler though not in any detail and in time I read that the head of counterintelligence had been arrested. I wondered if he was under suspicion, under arrest, or worse. Another thought occurred. Was Reinhard part of the crackdown? He was after all in the *Abwehr* and SS and the reports were that the *Abwehr* was disbanded. If so, I had placed the two army generals who consulted with me in grave danger. My word – no, my suspicion – was enough to have them tortured and put to death.

I simply did not know what to think anymore. Sleep was haunted by ferocious visions of fire and mass graves, this time with more clarity. I saw enormous flames racing across broad boulevards toward the Brandenburg Gate, graveyards as far as one could see with mangled faces flashing horribly before my eyes, men standing before a stone wall lit up by headlights awaiting death, and others killing themselves in chilly underground caverns oddly decorated with baroque furniture and candelabra.

In August a huge battle raged in France. Berlin boasted that fresh panzer divisions had been sent into the fray and results were promising. How confident that faithful voice was. But how correct was it? In a week it was clear that the battle was going in favor of the Allies. The BBC reported that tens of thousands of German prisoners had been taken near Caen and that German forces were in full retreat. Berlin stated that the Führer had made the strategically sound if not brilliant decision to fight from the border fortifications known as the Siegfried Line.

The Allies would soon be on German soil and I was elated.

REINHARD

My isolated life continued in my well-appointed cell with all my belongings and floors stained with blood. I went to the grocer's with my guard detail right behind me and sat in the park with them a bench away, relaxing with a smoke and talking about the war. It was the holiday season but their attention was on von Rundstedt's offensive in the west. It had driven deep into the American lines and they were sure it would turn the tide. I followed the news on the radio and felt it would do no such thing. I kept my counsel of course and wondered if Hitler would be calling for my services.

He did not and had not for over a year. Did he no longer find me useful? If that was the case, why did he not have me killed or cast me into Buchenwald until disease or a guard did the job. Perhaps he believed, or was told, that I had perished there already. But my dwelling was being paid for, deposits are made in my account, and the guards were outside at all times. My soul told me the wretch was not done with me – and that I was not done with him. Many hours were spent planning a future meeting.

At last Reinhard came by just before the New Year and my spirits were immediately lifted. We embraced lovingly the instant the door closed behind him. He brought tea and cheeses and wonderful bread, all fresh from Cologne. I scolded him for not bringing challah.

"Your mother's well. That's all I can tell you. I do not make visits or routine inquiries but I am confident she is well."

"Reinhard, you are a treasure! I cannot tell you how gratifying it is to know my mother is well, thanks to you. I would like to send her a letter in one way or another."

"Far too risky, dear. It would endanger whoever delivered it and the addressees as well. On the subject of letters...."

"Can we go to the park, please." I held his arm gently.

It was cold and the wind did not help matters but it was good to be outside and as much as we wanted to keep each other warm, we could not. The guards might think Reinhard and I were intimate despite being told we consulted on matters of state. In any case, proper people did not embrace in public in those days.

There were more maimed young men and elderly couples in suits and furs paraded about as though there were no armies were bombing and shooting each other, as though no camps were holding roll calls and selections. The good burghers of Munich made gallant shows of normalcy, perhaps because they knew that the next holiday season would be terribly different, if they were lucky enough to see it.

"I could not tell you face to face. I had to leave the letter. Looking you in the eyes and telling you of my role in your husband's death – in Joshua's death – would have pained me greatly. Furthermore, I wanted to leave you with a certain poignancy in case I never saw you again. After the assassination attempt, Berlin was in a fever. Hitler was badly wounded. His limbs are failing him and he cannot stay focused, save for one thing – revenge. Anyone even suspected of being a part of the attempt is arrested and tortured and put to death in horrifying ways. Some of the executions are filmed for his pleasure. No one is above suspicion. Not one. Aristocrats, generals, even famous ones. Did you hear of the great funeral for Field Marshal Rommel? He was involved in the plot."

"Yes. It was in the newspapers I recall his photograph and –. Reinhard! Please do not look surprised. The guards might sense something amiss. The general's face looked familiar but I thought it was from other reports about his accomplishments in North Africa. But I can place it now. He was one of the generals who came to me last summer before the invasion. There's no doubt in my mind.

Remember I sensed they were planning something criminal yet wonderful? That was it! They were planning to kill Adolf Hitler!"

"An impressive guest, dear, but you would do well to keep that information confidential in the event you have further important visitors."

"The newspapers and radio reports said he died as a result of wounds from being strafed in France."

"Rommel died by his own hand, though under pressure. Hitler adored Rommel. You could even say they were friends. Hitler gave him the opportunity to commit suicide. If he did not, he would put him to death along with his family. Alas, they failed and here we are speaking in hushed tones in a park."

"I would have expected military people to be skilled in killing people. It's their trade."

"Ach, someone moved the bomb at the last moment as I understand it. Hitler was spared, Germany was not."

"Nonetheless, they should have been able to kill one man. Hitler has a demonic quality. It makes him capable of great evil but also able to escape great perils. I felt that at more than one time. I also sense he will survive the catastrophe he created that will kill tens of millions of people before it is over."

"I hope you are wrong. My sense is that he will kill himself as the Allies near Berlin."

"I doubt it. There's some force protecting him. I sense it. Reinhard, these conspirators. What were their motives?"

"It's difficult to say with certainty. I cannot look into their hearts. Many were quite faithful to Hitler for many years, while we were winning. Rommel was a case in point. When defeat piled up on defeat they suddenly became patriots who wanted to save their Fatherland and saw him and his Nazi Party as stains on German honor that had to be removed. For over a year now, well over a year, the regular army has no longer been able to ignore what the Reich is doing. They know of the slaughter on the fronts and also the killings in the camps behind the fronts. Well, the Soviets will soon be in Poland and they will find four immense death camps and a hundred smaller ones."

"It's strange how the women in Buchenwald were able to go on day after day. They were horribly treated and poorly fed but they found ways to live. They told stories of their youths and laughed and prayed and wrote poetry in their heads. I was amazed."

"On the other side of that coin, the other *dreadful* side, the guards and *Aufseherinen* have picnics and dances on weekends. They even have a zoo where they can admire nature's work. It helps them get by and do their work day in, day out."

"What will Germany be like when this is over. Or will it ever be over?"

"The end will come within a few months. The armies coming at us are powerful and relentless. I see no reason they will not also be pitiless. They might agree to break Germany up into several smaller countries. Smaller and weaker. We will be as we were in the Middle Ages – a patchwork of small countries walked over by the powers. But, Bertha, you would know better than I what this country will be like in coming years."

"I see only rubble and graveyards and orphans in rags and stray dogs fighting over scraps of human flesh."

"Let's go home."

Two elderly men in uniforms from previous wars marched three dozen boys, no more than fourteen, into the park. The boys too were in uniforms though new ones like the ones worn by German soldiers in battle. The old men taught them to stand at attention and salute and march in formation. The boys' faces were bright and eager.

"They are in the *Volkssturm*. Berlin is mobilizing boys to send into battle."

"Hitler will throw away their lives too – the miserable wretch. Young boys, mere lads." I said. "Yes. Let's go home."

He stayed well into the night but forewarned me that he had to leave before dawn for appearance's sake. Shortly after midnight air raid sirens sounded with their low-pitch grinding noise rising and falling in pitch and volume and we heard the guards scurry into the cellar. Reinhard and I stayed put. An hour later the steady wail of all clear signal came. By then we were half asleep.

He returned a few day later for another short stay and by then we were more than a pair of lonely people seeking to ride out a storm. He had become my sole source of warmth and intimacy. Strange thoughts pass through the mind in time of war and isolation if only fleetingly, but for me there was the one thought that said he and I would not only survive, we would be together.

Amid a world of hatred two people, one a Jew, the other an officer in an organization devoted to eradicating every Jew in Europe, had fallen in love. It sounds terrible, I know, and the explanation will occur to many that a poor defenseless woman came under the sway of a man who professed to care for her but had less than honorable intentions. That was not the case. I loved Reinhard, and he loved me.

Just before dawn I awoke. I was again alone. The sound of the downstairs door closing came and I raced to the window. There was very little natural light and streetlights were of course not in use but I saw him walking down the street to the corner. I wanted to shout his name and get a final look but thought better of it. A black car soon arrived and as he entered he looked up at the window to me and waved. A beautiful moment, though one broken by the sinking sensation that I would never see him again.

TWILIGHT OF
THE GODS

The news in early 1945 was wonderful. Every broadcast was filled with news of steady Allied advances and German retreats. East and west, and to the south in Italy as well. The Americans and British were nearing the Rhine and the Russians were crossing the Vistula river. Beyond those to rivers lay straight paths Berlin.

Broadcasts from Berlin could not hide the advances, only add that the Führer had secret weapons and the tide would soon turn. That reminded me of the confident rural dwellers that we saw in a tavern and I wondered how many more portraits on the wall had black ribbons on them.

German cities and forests and farmlands are caught in a swift whirlpool, spinning faster and faster as millions shouted and screamed, before becoming twisted and unrecognizable and smaller, then sinking into a cold, silent oblivion.

The streets and parks of Munich were emptier. Many people had fled for smaller towns without war industries that were unlikely targets for the British and American bombers. Others simply stayed indoors, perhaps reluctant to show the fear in their faces which would sadden friends and cause the faithful to accuse them of insufficient patriotism. The grocer's shelves were emptying but the guards nonetheless brought me basic provisions, though I think they took some for themselves.

The end was coming and I wanted Reinhard to be with me. Whether we would perish in a bombing or be executed by one group of men or another, I did not know or care. The bizarre thought of the two of us setting out for the Swiss border occurred. Every morning came with the hope of seeing and even evening I slept alone. Day followed night, night followed day.

One morning I turned off the news and listened to music. The day was unusually pleasant. Rays of the sun came through clouds and warmed me as I sat at the table. I picked out a photograph album from the bookcase and leafed through images of schoolmates, neighbors, and relatives. In the back was one of my mother holding her newborn – me. We were gazing lovingly into each other's eyes. It was a wondrous photo of mother and child. An oceanic feeling swept over me.

Mother and child, mother and child, mother and child.

Can it be? Gently I touched my stomach.

In late February I was certain Reinhard's child was growing within me. Our baby would be born in a country in its death throes or in one that was becoming a new country. I hoped it would be a better one. I further hoped to be able to tell Reinhard the wondrous news.

Footsteps on the stairway awoke me. More than one person and Reinhard was not one of them. I donned a frumpy housecoat and opened the door. It was not the guard detail.

"Frau Siegelman, please pack a few things and come with us."

"Where are you taking –"

"You have one hour. Please be so kind as to pack for a day or two. You will be back before long, in all likelihood."

The "in all likelihood" was disconcerting but nothing was encouraging late in those days. I complied. What else could I do. Down the stairs we went and into a large black automobile, much more accommodating than Reinhard's to say nothing about what brought the new guards every eight hours or so.

"Are we going to Dachau?" I asked the officer beside me in the back.

He chuckled for a moment and replied, "No, no. If your destination was that place your vehicle would be much simpler and you would not have been asked to pack. We are going to the airport, then to Berlin."

That was a relief, of sorts. However, I knew whom I would be seeing, in all likelihood of course.

The airport was busy with military aircraft, taxiing on the tarmac, roaring on takeoff, gliding in for landing. Most of them looked to me like cargo planes rather than sleek fighter aircraft. We drove along the tarmac toward a large plane with rows of windows and three engines that were painted gold. The propellers were already spinning. On the tail was a swastika.

Shortly after the officer and I boarded we taxied down the runway and in a moment we were soaring over barren countryside and dark woodlands. The officer sat across the aisle and never looked my way. He had no idea what this was about and did not care. Orders.

Berlin from the air was horrifying. Large areas were in ruins and one had to look hard to find an area that had been spared. From the ground it was all the more so. Piles of rubble, some of them smoldering, were on every street. Rows of trees had been felled by explosions, their leaves and branches scorched by flames. People congregated on corners with looks of despair and fear. What was waiting for them. On one wall "The darkest hour is before dawn" had been hastily painted. Another one read "Victory awaits the valiant".

We headed for Charlottenburg, a fashionable old neighborhood in the city's western area, and came to a grand house whose wrought-iron gate opened the instant we neared it. It was an impressive dwelling, four stories, baroque in its gray facade and gables.

I was led to a salon with paintings of noblemen, tapestries of medieval markets, and Savonnerie carpets with intricacies I had never seen. The windows were covered in dark curtains and some of the furniture was draped. Plaster was missing from the ceiling but it had been swept up.

"You will wait here."

And wait I did for the better part of an hour until three figures appeared at the darkened top of a wide staircase with gilded bannisters on either side. One of them slowly and uneasily descended the stairs, holding the rail not out of caution but out of necessity. After a few steps there was sufficient light to know who it was. He limped to a red satin wing chair across from me, one arm stiff and held to his side, and slumped into the chair with a clump. No words, no eyes contact.

Hitler sat silently as thoughts and images pounded his head. He mopped his forehead and dabbed his nose with a handkerchief before stuffing it into the sleeve of his brown, double-breasted jacket. Once or twice he began to speak but stopped abruptly and mumbled unintelligibly. He suddenly stood remarkably swiftly and shouted at the top of his enfeebled lungs.

"Lies! Lies! Lies! I despise the stench of lies! Yet that is all I get from people! Lies! All around me! Lies!"

I was taken aback and feared for my life as much as I could after the ordeal of the last few years. He knew me to be a liar and called me in to accuse me, judge me, and put me to death in some gruesome manner. Pleading for my life would have gotten nothing and mention of a baby would have incited him to unspeakable things. I awaited the madman's verdict.

"You…. You…. You have always had confidence in me. You have always been sure of my unalterable will and of victory in the end. Not so with the generals around me! Disloyal, incompetent, and treasonous! Damn them all to hell! I have sent many there already and many more will follow!"

Relieved, I searched for words to continue the deception.

"My counsel has always been not to trust those around you. You will recall that. In my parlor, back in Munich, where you began your march."

He nodded and made uneasy eye contact with me. His eyes were dazed and more concerned with an inner world.

"I have one regret." I paused to get his attention on me. "I regret that when I warned you of your generals I neglected to give the name of the one you would never have suspected. The man who idolized you. The man you respected and trusted."

"Tresckow… Witzleben…."

"Not Tresckow. Not Witzleben. I speak of Rommel."

The name pierced him and he sat back down. He had indeed trusted Rommel but he was also astonished I knew of the Desert Fox's complicity, "Rommel! That scoundrel. I have his marshal's baton in my Chancellory. He is dead. That has been seen to. You are aware of it. Yes, you are aware of it. Of course you are."

His eyes looked downward while he mumbled and cleared his throat.

"That is in the past and it is done with. I did not bring you here to talk over old times like peasants in a tavern. What do you see ahead for my Reich?"

He looked at me hopefully, as though I controlled his future. I looked at him carefully, as though my life was at risk. If I told him all was lost would he have nodded, walked back upstairs, and shot himself? No. He would have killed me or shouted to the men darkling at the top of the stairs to do it. Had I suggested immediate surrender, he would have done the same. I leaned forward, still staring intently into him. I still had him.

"You are a most extraordinary man. I have long known that, but seeing you now and peering into your soul as you face your greatest trial has made me realize it all the more. Your destiny and Germany's are one and the same. They always were, they always will be. You knew that when you rose to power. You knew that when Poland and France bowed before you. You knew that when you lived through the bombing. You survived because more greatness is expected of you. You cannot walk away from your destiny. You cannot abandon Germany. Your deeds will ever be taught in schools far and wide. Your name will never be forgotten. Your sacrifices will never be forgotten nor will those made in your name. Yes, there is darkness all around."

He became disappointed, even unnerved.

"But remember, the darkest hour is just before dawn. Victory awaits the valiant!"

He was awed. The dazed eyes found focus and meaning for a

few moments and a faint, boyish smile came briefly across his pale countenance. I stared fiercely into his transfixed eyes. He could not have looked away if he wanted to or if a thousand air raid sirens suddenly wailed or if a million people screamed at once in horror. I knew his thoughts – and at that instant I was certain he knew mine.

You are a detestable monster who has killed millions. Your name will forever be stained by their blood. Germany will be broken into pieces and walked over by foreign armies.

Rage built inside him but subsided, erupted again, then fell away a second time. He could not comprehend what had just happened and more importantly he was weaker now than when he descended the stairs. He composed himself and glared back into my eyes.

I will survive this. I will endure. I will be renewed and revered for generations to come. I am the present, I am the future. My destiny and Germany's are one and the same.

He leaned back in the chair in exhaustion and mopped his brow again. He stood uneasily and looked to the two men coming down.

"Send her back to Munich! Now!"

I stood and walked toward the door, where the officer who took me here stood meekly.

"And Frau Siegelman, it is forbidden for SS officers to fornicate with Jews! There can be consequences."

The End,
the Beginning

As I boarded the plane at Tempelhof in the early evening there were flashes and reverberations to the east. The pilot and a crewman looked in that direction anxiously and consulted maps.

"The Russians are getting too damn close," the pilot said.

"We should stay in Munich. Better to be taken by the Americans than the Russians," the crewman added.

Well, in wartime America that was called "loose lips" but in Germany at the time it was no secret. Everyone knew the end was near and Stalin's wrath was to be feared. But of course had the Gestapo overheard them, they would have had to contend with their wrath, albeit only briefly.

Munich was even more deserted than a week earlier and when the staff car left me at my apartment there were no guards. They had either deserted or been attached to combat units. As good as it was to see them gone, the coming chaos concerned me. Gangs of youths could be seen along the streets breaking into buildings and shops looking for food and anything of value or simply smashing things for the sake of it.

At night I heard rumbling and looked to the west and saw flashes of light. The Yanks were coming as the song from the previous war had proclaimed.

I saw a few neighbors over the next few days but few wanted

anything to do with me. They smiled courteously rather than warmly or nodded briefly. They only knew I was kept under guard and had strange well-dressed visitors. They might also have heard gunshots and seen bodies taken out in the still of night.

The bombings had stopped as most of Munich had been leveled. The artillery was coming closer and a battle for every block was at hand. A storm was coming and I had to ride it out. I had a couple kilos of potatoes and onions and a tin of real tea. My building still had running water, though I took the precaution of filling the bathtub and a few containers. It would be enough to get by for a few weeks bunt no more than that. I prepared to bring some food, water, and bedding down to the cellar for the worst of it. I found myself saying several times a day, "The darkest hour is before dawn." Dark humor befitting the dark times.

One evening in mid-April I listened to the news. The main story was the death of Franklin Roosevelt. It was noted with solemnity in London, elation in Berlin. The reporter said this would break up the Allied coalition and turn the tide of war. He was either a good voice actor or extremely naive.

A music broadcast came on – Furtwängler conducting the Berlin Philharmonic. The musicians had evidently been forced to keep up appearances. The selection that evening was *Die Götterdämmerung* – The Twilight of the Gods. Richard Wagner had in some respects ushered in Nazism; now he was providing its funeral music.

I tried to envision mother. Where was she and was she safe. I closed my eyes and saw her no longer in a farmhouse but nonetheless alive. She was on a long trek. I felt her warmth, love, and spirit to live on.

Two weeks later the streets were empty. Cats and dogs scurried from alley to alley, garbage pail to garbage pail. The chirping of the birds was the only sound amid the eerily still urban landscape. The birds too fell silent and the small animals scurried down the street. Soon I heard what had alarmed them – motor vehicles, many of them. In front of them a handful of soldiers spaced about ten meters apart walked cautiously, looking side to side. White stars were on the vehicles. It was the Americans, the GIs, the Yanks.

I had been longing to see them for years and here they were. As much as I wanted to run out and embrace every one of them or cheer them on from a window, it was better to hold my piece lest they think me hostile, if only for a tragic, hurried moment.

Gunfire sounded every half hour or so but it was in the distance and the duration was brief. Munich was being liberated quickly and without a battle. Most of my fellow burghers probably breathed easier. American military police were much to be preferred over the Gestapo and the local police who had been taking orders from the Nazi hoodlums for years. Meanwhile reports from Berlin were of internecine fighting for every street and house.

Then came news that Hitler was dead. London reported it and Berlin confirmed it before going silent. I did not believe it. Hitler was alive somewhere. He got away from the Russians. I felt sure of it.

Loudspeakers crackled from jeeps. The German was quite good but with what I imagined to be more from Brooklyn than Brackenheim. It sounded lovely anyway. The burghers of Munich were ordered to assemble at a park, the very one I went to under guard and with Reinhard where I saw the old men teaching boys military basics. I wondered how many of them were killed their first day.

Nazi rule was over – in Munich and almost every part of Germany. Munich would be under American military authority for the time being. They promised to reestablish water and electricity, mail and telephone service, buses and trains, and to provide food when possible. Military police and intelligence offices would be set up to find people guilty of various types of crime. In time there would be an office to help find loved ones scattered by years of war, internments, and flight. I knew then that I would find my mother.

Each night I thought of her and went deep into the sea to try to determine where she was. She was alive though deeply weakened, not only after years at Buchenwald but from an arduous trek away from it. Each night brought slightly more information, slightly more certainty, slightly more assurance we would be reunited. She was not far away now.

The Americans opened an office where we could look for the names of loved ones and place our names on lists sent to other offices in Bavaria and later most of the areas controlled by the Yanks, British, and French. Mother's name was nowhere to be seen. I spoke with a young corporal from Baltimore whose German was decent and laced with Yiddish. His desk was cluttered with papers and manila folders, as were the dozen other desks in the room.

"Siegelman, Sonia Siegelman. That is her name. She is about fifty-five and tall for a woman. The last I knew my mother was in Buchenwald but that she left late in the war and traveled a great distance to another location."

The corporal was taken out of his ordinary routine for a moment. "How do you know that she left Buchenwald? Were you with her?"

"I was there for several months for upsetting an officer for one reason or another. They let me go and I have not upset an officer since, not one from any army."

"Hah! More than I can say! The officers in this place are easily upset. Tell you what. We will have rosters from the DP camps near Buchenwald in a few weeks."

"She is not near Buchenwald, I tell you. She walked a long way from that place."

"How the…. Just how do you know all this?"

"There is a bond between mother and daughter you will never understand. Even generals do not know of that bond or if they do they do not fully appreciate it. Are there DP camps near Dachau or near here?"

"Oh yes, quite a few." He rustled through some papers and handed me a list of small towns and villages around Munich. I scanned the list and had a sudden flash of knowledge.

"Föhrenwald!"

"What about Föhrenwald?"

"My mother is there."

"How the…. Is this another example of the mother-daughter bond that even generals cannot grasp?"

"It is. My mother is at Föhrenwald. I am certain of it. I am as certain of it as I am of your courtesy and intention to help me reach my mother."

"I am a corporal, not a general. Thank heaven."

"But you know how to get things done. I can see that."

"Come back on…" He looked at a calendar on the wall across the room. "Monday morning. I can have the Föhrenwald roster by then."

"You are going there yourself."

"What?"

"You're going there yourself – by jeep."

"How the…."

I arrived Monday morning with a valise and waited in line to see the corporal but he was nowhere to be seen. I looked around and waited but still could not find him.

"Frau Siegelman!" finally came my name from the back of the room. The Yiddish-speaking corporal was waving to me. "This way. This way, please."

"Did you get the Föhrenwald roster?"

"Not yet. The mail is lousy. But I can drive there this morning to pick it up. Naturally, I will need someone –"

"You will need someone who knows the roads and speaks German better than you."

"Correct again." He escorted me to behind the building where sat a jeep. "Hop in, ma'am. You do know the roads, don't you?"

"Not in the slightest but we will get there all the same. And my German is vastly better than yours but you're a fast learner."

"You know, I think if I asked you who was going to win the World Series you could tell me."

Off we went driving south through countryside that became hilly and eventually mountainous. It was an idyllic Germany that I was pleased to see had survived. I was in heaven knowing I was on my way to see mother.

In an hour we came upon the camp. It had a barbed wire perimeter and a few guard towers but was not nearly as sinister and depressing as Buchenwald. The corporal talked with the guards at the checkpoint in rapid English, then headed for an administrative building. He was down there and chatted jovially with a few other corporals and privates. It was about baseball, I believe. Finally, a young private sat us down with the roster. It must have been fifty pages.

"Sonia Siegelman," I spelled it out for him. "She was at Buchenwald and lived in Munich before that."

They leafed through page after page until they came to the names starting with an S.

"No Siegelman here. Sorry."

"Are you spelling it correctly? I am quite certain she is here."

"How is she certain?" the private asked after my corporal-driver translated.

"Never mind. Let's just look through it again."

I peeked as they ran down the names.

"There it is! You misspelled her name. There is an 'e' in our name!"

"Well, it *might* be her. It says here she's assigned to Building B412. She's a teacher in our school here."

"Does she teach music?"

He looked at a map of the camp.

"Yeah. B412 is where we teach children to play music."

The three of us were off down rows of barracks with neatly trimmed grass between them, each stenciled with a designation. The buildings were obviously rapidly put up and appeared about as sturdy as the ones in the camp I was in, but they did not have the oppressive, despairing feel to them. Many of the people showed signs of lingering malnourishment and for some optimism was yet to return to their faces. But they walked about happily and freely. No fearsome Kapos or guards.

Music! I heard music from a building not fifty meters away! A piano was playing. Eager as I was to see mother again I did not want to interrupt her class. I stood quietly just inside the door while my escorts obligingly stayed outside. She was playing "Fur Elise," a delicate but simple Beethoven piece. The children were rapt. God knows what they had been through over the last few years and how many had lost mothers but they loved the music. When the short piece was over I applauded as loud as I could and mother looked over in utter disbelief. As we embraced and wept the children clapped their hands and cheered.

Many had lost mothers.

Paperwork, paperwork, and more paperwork. It took a mountain of paperwork to get mother out of the camp but forms came in and then sent back. Upon approval mother was reluctant to leave the children behind. But a new teacher was found in short order and she was off to Munich by bus. Apprised of her arrival, I met her at the depot next to the train station and back to my townhouse we went. Her house had been sold a few years ago and there was a lengthy procedure to get it back. More paperwork.

We walked about the city for hours. Most of it was in ruins. That was the case with the opera house.

"It was destroyed in the early nineteenth century," mother recalled from the city's history. "It was rebuilt a few years later. Munich needed it to be considered a great city like Paris and Rome. I suppose the opera house in Berlin has met the same fate as ours."

"It probably has been destroyed as well. They can be rebuilt. People need something to link them to their past though of course there is much in our recent history that few will want to recall."

"No, Bertha, few will be able to forget it. So many deaths, so much cruelty. History goes on."

"Yes! History is going on right now, all around us. It needs to be written down. Munich has been destroyed and it will be built up again. There is a story there and I can write it."

"If you have your father's Leica you can photograph it all."

"I do have it stashed away. I wanted to use it during the war but 35mm film was impossible to find. It probably still is."

"Bertha, my stay in Föhrenwald showed me that Americans have everything in their army stores, PXes. Supply sergeants are royalty, the new Wittelbachs of Bavaria. But you'll need money."

"I have quite a bit of it stashed away. I can convert it to GI scrip."

"You have a mission, Bertha. You are the chronicler of Munich in the year zero."

"The university will be reopening in a year. I know it!"

I picked up a piece of rubble the size of my thumb and put it into my pocket. Mother and I went out for walks almost every day and my collection grew.

Food became available after a month or so and we did not have to live on potatoes and what the American authorities provided which was as often as not C Rations. I don't recommend them and I felt sorrow for the GIs who had to get by on them for so long. Mother and I made do.

I resumed my career as a seer. There were so many people searching for lost loved ones who had been in the military or who had been swept up by the Gestapo. I seldom found reason for hope.

So many people had been pulled down into the whirlpool of war and terror.

A small number of GIs sought my help. They wanted to know what lay ahead for America and for them once they returned home after years in Europe. One man was a captain in a criminal investigation section charged with tracking down war criminals and gathering evidence for prosecutions. I had suspicions as to why he visited me.

Mother and I sat in the parlor after dinners and spoke of the present and future far more than of the past. The university would reopen in the spring of 1946 and she would be able to get her professorship back. Most faculties had several professors and *dozents* killed in Gestapo roundups or the camps or the bombings. Some were fortunate to have simply grown old and retired. I planned to return to graduate work and become a lecturer. There was an issue hanging over our evenings, one that time was making essential to discuss.

"Mother, I am expecting. I am carrying a baby."

She quickly and silently determined that Joshua was not the father.

"Bertha, were you...."

It was a common enough thing during the war and its chaotic aftermath. Men on the verge of defeat and death, men on the wave of victory and departure, can both feel a sense of entitlement with lone women.

"No, mother, thankfully that was not the case. I was alone and so was he and we found a measure of humanity when we were together. In time there was a feeling of intimacy. I do not know where he is now. It was late in the war and there was so much confusion and violence. And, mother, sometimes people who seem heartless are not."

It was quite a bit for her to take in. A few swallows of tea and a gaze out the window helped.

"We have all been through an ordeal and seen so many lives ruined and ended. Your child will be part of a new world and a much better one too and I look forward to helping you raise the welcome addition to our family."

"Oddly, mother, my gift is of no help in discerning my own baby's gender."

"We shall have to wait and see. It will be wonderful to look forward to learning the news!"

That was it. A burden had been lifted and my soul was at peace. A pregnant single woman before the war was a disgrace. Parents were outraged and ashamed. The wayward girl had to be sent off somewhere and the child put up for adoption far away. The war made those conventions out of step and the need to band together to survive put old ways in the ash heap. I would have my baby in about five months and he or she would have a loving mother and grandmother.

I would no longer have to conceal my growing tummy from mother.

An "uncomplicated" Birth

I n the fall I was heavy with child as the expression went. I was the university speaking with the faculty about returning to the doctoral program when I broke water and was taken to the university hospital not far away. Men were coming and going on crutches or limping badly. Some had missing arms and wore eyepatches. More than handful had a dazed, despairing look. Paradoxically, I had seen that same look on people in Buchenwald.

My contractions were not close so I was placed in room with another woman about to give birth. Nina was her name. We passed the time and intermittent pains by chatting. At first we spoke about wanting a boy or a girl. She said she wanted a girl and made the sign of the cross. We talked about what part of Munich we lived in, the doctors and nurses at the hospital, and where to buy baby clothes and the like. It was enjoyable, all things considered, and probably two hours went by. The pain continued and the nurses said we were still hours away from motherhood. Nine and I continued to talk, with more and more frankness. We should have stuck to lighter subjects.

"Have you seen the news about those awful trials in Nuremberg?" she said in anguished tones.

"Yes, I have. Everyone is following the news yet I cannot bear to follow the matter too closely. Far too distressing."

"Ugh! I feel the same way about them."

A pause came. I had thought everyone was in agreement on Nuremberg, but that wasn't the case.

"Do you know anything about those camps, Bertha?"

"I spent several months at Buchenwald."

"So you are a Jew," she said in a cold tone. She turned her head to the window even though there was nothing especially attractive about the gray building not thirty meters away.

I saw her in girlish braids, her eyes moistening as she cheered Brown Shirts marching to martial tunes on Brienner Strasse. This was part of their support. Not evil, merely naive.

"You know, Bertha, Hitler did many good things for Germany. Our factories were running again. Our men had good jobs. We were able to hold our heads up proudly again because we stood up to the British and the French and the Bolsheviks. So many good things. You will never hear them even mentioned at those trials. Not once."

"Those men are on trial for imprisoning innocent people, torturing them, starving them, and killing them. Millions of people. Millions of them. Even children and babies!"

"Yes, yes. That's what the occupying armies tell us in their radio broadcasts and newspapers. I never saw any of those things. Hitler went too far, I admit that. He never should have invaded the Soviet Union. It is too big and too cold!" She giggled.

Stalingrad…mass grave. Stalingrad…mass grave.

"The rest of what he did might have gone too far as well but he was a good German. You wait. In a few years when these armies are gone and we can be ourselves again Germany will take another look at the Nazi years. For now, oh for now we have to watch what we say. Right, Bertha?"

"We certainly do. Have you read about the trains packed with people, the gas chambers, the crematories?"

"Yes, of course. That is what I mean by the foreign armies controlling the information we have. They force us to believe all that. I simply don't believe it."

"It's true. Talk to people who were there. Women who were about to give birth were put to death, Nina."

"Oh, that never happened! No German man would do such a thing! You surprise me, Bertha. You really do."

"I saw men hanging by their necks for days. I saw women raped. Pregnant women were put on trains for Auschwitz. One of them was shot dead. German men did those things, Nina. There is a dark part in the human soul."

"Bertha, I am sorry you feel these things but my husband tells me they are lies spread by those who want Germany to be weak again. I do not want to upset you, not at this moment."

"My husband was shot dead before my eyes, Nina. You are right though. We must talk about more cheerful things."

"I am sorry you lost your husband but I am glad he left you with a gift."

She smiled with a warmth I did not think possible from one so naive and misguided. I did not want to go on about the Nazis or reveal who my baby's father was. That bit of information would have been processed in her mind as evidence of the SS's good-heartedness.

Instead, I returned her warm smile and gaze until a dread feeling swept over me. the kind that makes me wish I never had my gift.

Death…her baby will not live. Poor child, poor woman.

A nurse came by to check on us and found all our vital signs were good but my sense of imminent trouble deepened.

"Nina, please take my hand!"

She was touched and immediately reached over to me.

A boy…something wrong…something very wrong.

"What is it, Bertha? Are you in pain?"

"Nina, I have certain senses that are hard to explain. Ask the nurse to call your husband. He should get here as soon as possible."

"But my contractions aren't close! My husband's shift is just beginning."

"Please trust me, Nina. Get word to him anyway you can. I know certain things. You must believe me."

"You know what? You see what others cannot? Is that why you took my hand? Is that why you took my hand? Is there something wrong? Oh my God, you know something terrible will happen to my baby! What's going to happen to my baby? Tell me! Tell me!"

She summoned the nurse with a bell on the night table and asked her to get in touch with her husband as soon as possible. The nurse saw no great need but nonetheless assured her she would have her husband called. Try as I did to conceal it, the sorrow and trepidation on my face were clear and anything I said to calm her would only have caused more consternation.

"Is my baby going to die? Am I going to die? Oh God, please not both of us!"

"Nina, please do not panic. Yes, I feel certain things but I am not always correct. I simply think it best your husband be here with you."

Her pleading eyes and my increasing pain and exhaustion made stop any pretense.

"Oh Nina, poor Nina, poor Nina, I hope I am wrong, I hope I am terribly wrong."

We held hands again and cried for an hour until her husband arrived. The nurse closed the curtain between our beds and I listened to their whispers and whimpers until she was taken to the delivery room. Sleep took me.

I was awakened by the sound of the nurse opening the curtain divider and there was Nina beaming, her husband beside her, as she held their newborn.

"This is my son. Isn't he wonderful?"

"He is beautiful! I am very happy for you and your husband!"

I was relieved. Perhaps I had been mistaken. Perhaps my own fears had influenced my perceptions of others. My own pains were worsening and I wanted a return to slumber, but a sense of dread hung over me.

When I awoke Nina was gone and a practical nurse was changing the bedding for a new expectant mother. When I asked about Nina, the sad expression told the tale. Not long thereafter, Nina's husband told me the baby had died suddenly and the mother had just been taken to a private room before she would be discharged.

"Thank you for having me summoned. I do not know how you sensed trouble but we are grateful you did. Nina and I were able to share the few hours of our baby's life."

"Oh, we women have our ways of knowing."

"I am not sure how much you spoke with her. She likes to express her views on things. There was a time we agreed on almost everything. That was before the war. I hope she said nothing to upset you and I hope you have a fine, healthy baby."

He limped noticeably as he left and amid my intermittent pain I wanted to know how he came by it. The answer came to me suddenly.

"Were you at Berlin when the end came?"

"Yes. Yes, I was there. Fortune was with me and my battalion was able to get out to the west where we surrendered to the Americans. But how did you…ah, you women have your ways."

The pains became sharper and came closer together and every young woman knows that means the prelude is over and the main event is at hand. At last, my baby was coming. The staff concurred and I was wheeled to the delivery room down a brightly-lit corridor where nurses tended to me in a routine but comforting manner. I lay back and felt the pain become the warmth of impending motherhood. A bad feeling came which I initially thought was lingering sadness over Nina's baby or a sense of responsibility for complicity but a clarity came to me that excluded past events. Something bad was coming, soon, and in that delivery room.

The doctor came in and scrubbed up. He and the nurses were perfectly calm. They'd done this a hundred times, I told myself. Trust them, not the panicked senses of a new mother. Pain distracted me. Child birth can be like that, focusing your mind on it and promising an amazing reward. I felt the baby making its way out, then halting, taking a break, reconsidering things.

The doctor said the baby's feet were first and he had to perform a manual procedure to turn it. He did it immediately and birth came in less than minute.

"You have a daughter, Bertha!" the nurse said, rather unemotionally.

I lay in a blissful daze, desperate to see my baby. Something was wrong though. The doctor and the nurse were trying to get my daughter to breathe and begin life. Their efforts went on and on.

"Is something wrong? Is something wrong? I have to know!"

"The umbilical cord was wrapped around the baby's neck and the birth is complicated," said the doctor taking a moment from an obviously urgent situation.

I felt things slipping away. Light was fading, warmth giving way. I knew my child was not going to live.

"My fault! All my fault for helping them," I cried.

"Nothing is your fault, Bertha," said a nurse as she held my hand. "We're doing everything we can. Please believe that."

"I helped them! And this is my punishment!"

The nurse looked over to the others as they continued to work on my baby. Still no breathing, still no motion. The effort continued but the urgency was diminishing. The doctor and nurses looked at each other.

"We did everything we could, Bertha. I swear to you we did. You must not blame yourself. I cannot imagine anything anyone could have done to be punished like this," the doctor said consolingly.

I could easily imagine what I had done to deserve this. Had I expressed any of this to them at that moment they would not have believed me and worse, they might have placed me in a special ward. I began to think the mere presence of Hitler and others of his ilk poisoned me and this was a way of not only punishing me but of cleansing me and allowing me go on, chastened and permanently stricken.

"Let me hold her. I need to be with her for a while.

Mother and child, mother and child, mother and child.

The doctor nodded and a nurse lay my baby girl on top of me, her head near my breast. Such innocence and sweetness! I whispered that I loved her and was so sorry for what I had done and would give up my own life to let her live. I tried to send my being into her in that hope. I closed my eyes and thought of nothing but giving life to my baby. I thought of my mother and her ordeals and of the poor women in the camps who did not have the chance to have children or who did give birth and lost their babies in monstrous ways.

I wanted my baby to live and felt myself starting to die, but I was drifting into the sea, deeper than I'd ever been. A name came to me.

"Nadia...Nadia. I am your mother, but you know that. I want you to live and grow up to be a good woman in a better world. Nadia, I love you. I love you with all my heart. Nadia, please hear me. Please live. Please."

Mother and child, mother and child, mother and child.

I felt Nadia's spirit, her essence, her very being. Yes, I felt it. And if I felt it, she was not truly gone. She was within reach. I felt her moving back from darkness and inching toward me.

"Yes, Nadia! I am here, Nadia! Breathe, Nadia! Breathe!"

A soft gurgling sound caused me to open my eyes and I saw her lips move if only slightly. More gurgling. more motion! Nadia was coming to me! I looked around and saw the doctor and nurses were gone.

"Nurse! Nurse! Please come immediately! My baby is alive!"

She scurried in expecting to have to calm me and say it was all my imagine and prepare a sedative.

"Oh, my God! She's alive! The baby's alive! Get the doctor back here!"

They worked on her and got her to breathe more easily. Removing a little mucous from the nose and throat did the trick. The nurse threw out the old paperwork and filled out a live-birth record.

"Nadia. Her name is Nadia."

"Nadia it is. And welcome to the world, you brave little girl!"

That evening mother was allowed in to see me and her granddaughter. She held Nadia as lovingly as she assuredly held me so many years ago.

"She's perfect, Bertha! Did the birth go well?"

"Oh, there was a complication but nothing more than that. Let's talk about it when we're home – the three of us."

Nadia brought hope and focus and new love to our home. Mother and I doted on her at home and paraded her about the streets and parks. Children without fathers were no rarity. I wondered how I would explain to her who her father was and the circumstances of our meeting. That was a long way off.

Actually, I never did tell her.

Munich was coming back to life. Shops were reopening, goods were back on shelves, and people walked about without the looks of despair that had for the previous two years. They now looked determined. I was attending classes at the university and serving as a teaching assistant to a professor who agreed to supervise my doctoral work on postwar Munich. I took on fewer clients in my old business but retained a small number, including a GI I felt was in counterintelligence.

Mother, Nadia, and I began attending *Schul* at a new synagogue. The rabbi had survived the war and often spoke of his ordeal and the survival of tradition. We were not religious but we wanted a sense of community and belonging, for ourselves and our little girl. We found it. I never felt entirely at home there. I was never especially religious and I could never explain adequately why I spent only a few months at a camp. Nor could I reveal my wartime clients or who Nadia's father was.

The rabbi often spoke of Jewish people leaving Europe and settling in Palestine, often on communal farms, or *kibbutzes*. It appealed to mother and me and we talked about going there even though lives as farmworkers were not attractive. "The kibbutzes will need teachers," mother said. "So will the whole country."

We could never feel entirely at home in Germany. Its past was never completely gone. Nazis and war criminals were still being found and I often felt I was not entirely done with what I had done. Those meetings with dark figures haunted me day and night. Germany's future was clouded by the prospect of foreign occupation for many years. Palestine was a new land, one that might become a Jewish state. That was intriguing.

THE HUNTERS

A man came by one morning when mother was away and Nadia was sleeping soundly. I could see from his attire he was not a tradesman selling goods door-to-door and his accent told me he was from well north of Munich, perhaps Hamburg. I sensed no malevolence, only an austere demeanor of someone on official business.

"Frau Siegelman, I wish I had been able to call ahead for an appointment but I only learned of your special abilities last night. Ach, we work such long hours."

"That is understandable, Herr...."

"Walter. Stefan Walter."

"How did you learn of my special abilities?"

"Another time perhaps."

"You are with an investigative body."

That took him aback though it strengthened my reputation. Who had sent him, I wondered. Was it that American officer who came into my parlor from time to time? Someone at the synagogue?

"I am indeed with an investigative organization, an extraordinary one charged with bringing a certain category of criminals to justice."

"Nazis."

"Yes. The Nuremberg Trials dealt with the high-ranking Nazis – Göring, Hess, and the like."

A folder with my name on it in red ink. A file drawer with the same. No!

Was there a dossier somewhere in Berlin with my name and a list of my clients? Was I to help the hunter or am I the hunted?

"Hitler had countless helpers at middle and lower levels. Our task is to find them and bring them to justice and we believe you can help."

"I fail to see how I can be of help. I am a student and lecturer, not a lawyer. And I have a young child, whom I suspect you already know of."

"You are being too modest, Frau Siegelman. You have exceptional gifts of, well, judging people, seeing what dwells inside them, and what roads they take. I would like you to come to our office in the new part of Munich. We bring suspects there, ask questions – interrogate them, if you will – and make preliminary judgments about their guilt or innocence and about further investigation. We seek to use as many tools as we can, including the ones you possess, which I add you have ably demonstrated to me this morning."

"I would like to help you. As a German and a Jew I feel bound to help. However, you know of the true believers who have not given up and have a clandestine organization."

"The Werewolves. Odessa."

"Yes, and others. I must have assurance that my identity will be kept strictly confidential – for my safety and that of my mother and daughter."

"You have my assurance of complete confidentiality. I hope we can begin later this week."

"I look forward to it."

I did not look forward to it in the least. A sense of duty was in my heart but intermingled with fear he had something on me. I dreamed of dossiers with my name on them – hundreds of them, piles of them.

Stefan called me one day and said a car would be set for me in the morning and we went for the newer part of Munich where brutalist office buildings had been built. As I was about to get out of the car I donned a dark scarf that partially covered my face. Inside Stefan introduced me to the handful of people in his section. Most were young people. Two were lawyers and one of those was Jewish. I sensed he had been in a camp. I further sensed that my presence was not wanted by everyone. At least one thought I was a fraud and the whole thing was a waste of time. On the desk was a pile of dossiers.

I was briefed on procedures and given dossiers with affidavits and photos. When the time came I sat in a small, bare room with only a small table and two office chairs. Next door was one or more members of Stefan's section, listening in, taking notes, waiting to bring the boss good news. Rarely was I able to get a detainee to incriminate himself. Most of them had prepared stories and were able to stick to them. No evidence, no witnesses, no case.

Stefan apprised me one afternoon of a man in an interrogation room down the hall. He was twenty-five but had no paperwork to indicate he had been in the army or had worked in the civilian world. The man said he worked in various factory jobs and all his papers were lost when he was robbed by deserting soldiers.

"Plausible," Stefan said. "But suspicious. Sit with him. Peer inside him. Try to irk him into saying something we can charge him with or look into. I have a feeling about this one. Not your kind of feeling, Bertha,"

"You never know," I replied impishly.

"What I mean is that my section has been at this for over a year now and we have developed a certain judgment about people. We have two inmates at Dachau who believe he was guard there, and a rather brutal one, even a murderous one. Alas, they are uncertain and without their certainty –"

"You cannot take him to court."

"Hence my car at your door today, Bertha!"

I sat with the suspect in a darkened room.

"Who are you?" he snapped. "You're not one of them."

"I am one of them when I want to be one of them. And today I want to be one of them. My name is Siegelman."

He all but sneered at the name and I felt his deep hostility toward my people. I peered into him. He did not welcome it but he could not stop it. Nor could he prevent images and ideas from flowing out of his dark soul.

"And I of course know your name, Herr Webern. There is a remarkable gap in your whereabouts during the war years and some here find that highly suspicious. I am not one of them, I can assure you! Still, there are questions I must ask."

I asked several questions about what factory he worked at and what was made there and who his supervisor was. He knew something about a steel mill in the Saar Valley but nothing of the plant's layout.

"Were there Jews working there? Slave laborers, I mean."

"Maybe. I'm not sure. It was so long ago!"

"It must have been hard work. Too hard for me! Do you believe that work makes you free?"

That was the motto on Dachau's main gate – and he knew it!

"Ah, so you know of Dachau then."

"I have read of it. There were many Jews there."

He was a guard there. At roll calls and selections. More.

"But you were there! I am certain of it. Do not ask how I know such things. We know. The evidence is clear. It's all here!"

I pointed to his dossier on the desk but didn't open it.

"There were many guards who simply did their duty."

"So you *were* a guard at Dachau."

"Only briefly."

He shot an old man who was late to roll call.

"Then you must know of roll calls and work details."

"Yes. They were part of the routine."

"And the routine had to be followed by all."

"Yes, of course. By all. Those were the rules."

"It would be understandable for someone who arrived late and broke the rules to be punished." This hit home. He was nervous and increasingly angry. "If you are late you have to be punished. The routine, the schedule, the rules. That goes for old people too. That goes for old Jews too!"

"Especially for old Jews! Especially for old lazy Jews!"

"You had to do it. You had to enforce the routine, the schedule, the rules. You had to kill him!"

He erupted in a tirade against me and Jews and went on to describe the insolence of the old man and his look of surprise when the first bullet struck. He lunged at me but thankfully Stefan was just outside. He and another rushed in to subdue him.

"Goddam Jews!" he shouted. "I wish I had killed more. One day everyone will know we were only doing that had to be done. You are a Jew witch! A Jew witch! Hear me?"

"I have been called a Jew witch by men of higher station than you. He was at Buchenwald, however. And then there was a man in Berlin. Goodbye, young man."

One fellow I was certain was a criminal and I wrote s brief report articulating my reasoning. Stefan and the team went to work and discovered the man had been in a regular army unit with no cases of atrocity attached to it. I might have been seeing evil and criminality in every man I met and I did not think I could be of any help.

Stefan pushed me on to do one more interview and I reluctantly accepted. He handed me a folder and I opened it and saw the name in bold print – Reinhard Beck.

My heart raced. A flood of memories came to me but the name was not uncommon and I looked through the material and came upon three photographs. One was a graduation photo from the Berlin officers academy, the other two were from the *Abwehr*, the Reich's counterintelligence bureau. It was him alright.

What to do? I could not tell anyone he was the father of my baby or that he had he had been an intermediary between Hitler and me. Or was Stefan setting me up? He might have already known all that. Reinhard might have told him that information to get himself out of trouble.

"Which room is he in?" I asked calmly.

We walked down the empty hallway to one of the interrogation rooms. Stefan waited outside as usual. Reinhard knew me instantly and comprehended that we had to play roles here. He was a suspect and I an investigator and the days and nights together had to be pushed into back recesses for now. He banished his look of recognition and I sat across the table from him.

"Herr Beck," I began in official tones, "you were a mid-level officer in the SS. Where were you stationed and what was the nature of your work?"

Reinhard broke free of the men arresting him and charged with executing him. He hid out for the rest of the war at his aunt's home near Erfurt.

"After training in Berlin I was assigned to oversee construction of the Buchenwald camp as it was going to be used as a prison for communists. That only lasted a few months, until about 1937. I applied for a transfer to the *Abwehr* in Berlin and was pleased when it was approved."

"I am sure that was challenging work."

He went on for almost thirty minutes on seeking Soviet agents in the government and business sectors, mainly in Bavaria. I sensed it was true but his presentation seemed prepared like the lines of prospective employee at the hiring office. There was an underground network called Odessa that helped former SS personnel hide their identities, evade the authorities, and even escape to South America. Reinhard had been in contact with Odessa though I could sense no criminality or evil.

"And you now work for BMW?"

"Yes. I am happy to say I have adjusted to the new Germany and hope to manage a motorcycle plant that will be opening next year."

A thought came to me and I riffled through the dossier but found no answer.

"You are married, are you not?"

He was briefly dismayed but recovery was swift.

"Yes. I married a woman I knew before the war. That was only a year ago."

"And you are a father now."

He smiled softly and sweetly, unsure how I came upon that knowledge.

"Yes. We had a baby boy just four months ago. We're very happy."

"I can see that. Well, I have a daughter of my own now. She is a year old. It is amazing how quickly things have happened since the war."

Reinhard thought it through and came to a realization. He was unnerved by the possibilities before him in that room. Would malevolence lead me to punish him? Would I hound him in his new life for years on end?

"That will be all, Herr Beck. I am sure this process will be over for you soon and then you can go about your new life with your wife and child – as can I with my daughter Nadia."

"Nadia… That's a lovely name. My son is named Abraham."

My heart skipped a beat. It was my father's name.

"Abraham. A fine name. It suggests longevity and strength."

"May that be the case for us and our families."

"Abraham was my father's name."

"Ahh. An even better name than I thought. I hope he grows up to be as good a man as your father surely was."

He nodded and smiled again. We wanted to embrace before I left. I'm sure of it. That couldn't be done under the circumstances. Besides, there was a finality to our last, bittersweet words. We had made a silent pact. The war and its convolutions were in our pasts. I smiled back, picked up his dossier, and left the room.

"I sensed no criminality in this one, Stefan. In fact I sensed he's had learned a great deal over the last few years."

I walked out of the building for the last time and went home to my family. I sensed I'd never see Reinhard again but I felt the same when I saw him get into a black car and drive off late in the war. As it turned out, I never did see him again, yet he'll always be in my heart.

THE BUNKER

I felt free of past associations and open to a new ones. My doctoral research took a great deal of time, as did little Nadia, and Munich was not replete with eligible men in those years. The war and Holocaust had seen to that. I spent most of my evenings with mother and my little girl. Life was warm and loving, more than I could have hoped.

I began work as a *dozent* in the fall of 1947. I taught a survey course on western civilization for incoming freshmen and a course based on my doctoral research on Munich during and after the war. Students were mostly too young to have served in the war. There were a few I sensed had been in uniform in their early teens and were badly scarred by the experience. I understood why they took my course on Munich and why they tended to sit in the back and not ask questions.

After a lecture on the fall of Berlin one of the young veterans knocked on my office door. I beckoned him to come in and sit. He was all of eighteen and had the eyes and soul of a man fortune had not favored. His eyes had seen too much and I pitied him. He had difficulty making eye contact.

"Frau Siegelman, I enjoy your lectures. As you may know I am in both your classes. My question is perhaps impossible to answer but the thoughts of someone who lived through the war and studied it would interest me."

He paused and looked downward.

"It sounds like a thoughtful mind has come up with a challenging question. Go on. Please."

"Everyone talks about the Nazi period being over and a new Germany emerging. I wonder though, could the Reich come back? There is such evil in men's hearts. A lust for war and glory and dominance. These things are in us, waiting for the opportunity to come back."

I asked myself the same question countless times and arrived at no firm position.

"I see the past quite well. It's my profession. I cannot see decades into the future. My horizon is limited. The future of Germany will be formed by people who indeed have those things in their hearts. They also have the Reich's evil seared into their memories, and that can be liberating. I hope you see that."

An uneasy smile came briefly across his youthful face like the sun on a somber day. I studied his face, hopefully not imposingly.

Three boys in oversized military tunics scurrying from one pile of rubble to another. Tracer bullets streak at them and two of them fall. The third hides behind a burned panzer with a black hole in its turret.

"Were you in the *Volkssturm* at the end of the war?"

"How did you know? Is it in my records?" he asked worriedly.

"No, your records do not have any such information. I, well, have a gift for such things."

"I have something like that. I can see it on faces."

By 1950 my little family was doing very well Mother was a tenured professor once again. I completed my doctorate and was a lecturer in the history department but salaries were quite low and I began doing some readings once more. The business throve and in a year I was earning a good deal more than I did at the university. After two years we moved into a large house with a yard and a view of the Isar River. It was a short, pleasant walk to the *Alte Pinakothek* which was being rebuilt as a great art museum. There was a new spirit in Germany but the concern of that young veteran came to mind periodically, as did Hitler's last message.

I will survive this. I will endure. I will be renewed and revered by future generations. I'm the present, I am the future.

A noted British professor came to the university to give a lecture on his book about the end of the Third Reich. I attended. He was a tweedy fellow with thick glasses and long unkempt hair. He scoffed at notions that Hitler was still alive. Hitler, he concluded after considerable research in recent years and considerable bluster that day, had committed suicide in a Berlin bunker as Soviet troops closed in. Claims to the contrary were Stalinist propaganda that also asserted that Hitler was being held by the western powers for nefarious purposes against the Soviet Union.

The audience rewarded him with polite applause. They found his findings convincing and soothing. I did not. I walked briskly back home, startling people as I muttered, "He's alive. I know it. He's alive."

At home I knew something was coming. I barely touched my dinner and listened to Furtwängler from Berlin. Wagner was very much out of favor. Sibelius's "Swan of Tuonela" was played with the conductor's idiosyncratic tempi applied to the haunting tone poem based on Swedish myth.

I dreamed of the early days when Brown Shirts handed out flyers on street corners and played patriotic music. A gust of wind blew a flurry of leaflets at me. Some of them stuck to my coat, others flew into my face, blinding me. I brushed them away frantically and saw them coming at me and growing into giants. "We remember you," one of them gloated as he grabbed my dress. I ran to a wire fence and grabbed hold until my shrieking woke me up.

Fortunately, mother and Nadia were away in the mountains for a week. I decided to discern what I could about Hitler's fate. I locked all the doors and closed the drapes. I fasted for two days and nights. Nothing but water and the only light came from candles.

Munich was silent after midnight, all the more so by 3am. That's when I closed myself off from the world and immersed myself in the sea. "Berlin...Berlin...Berlin," I whispered. There was no need to offer a time. A train rumbled out of Munich in the dark distance. I felt nauseated as I floated away.

Berlin — parts in ruins, others in flames. More thunder, closer thunder. A courtyard was below me some thirty meters. The building was badly damaged. A man, woman, six young girls, and a boy were lying on the ground as soldiers poured petrol on them and set them ablaze. The smoke swirled skyward toward me and I had to evade it so that I could see.

There was Hitler beside the burning corpses, quiet, detached, remorseless, occasionally looking up when a roaring sound roared overhead. He was not in his Nazi party attire. Nor was he in a suit or military garb. He was in the gray gabardine jacket and pants of a working man and could be mistaken for a deliveryman or a plumber or stock clerk in a store. Four men in similar clothing crept with him away from a shrapnel-scarred building and exterior wall. He was limping badly and an arm swung uselessly with each step. They scurried as best they could across a boulevard, heading south and stopping at a pile of rubble as an artillery round came overhead before impacting not forty meters away with a terrifying cracking sound. Hitler thought back to the trenches of the previous war.

They headed south and at times mingled with bedraggled soldiers and beggars and madmen. Their journey lasted hours until they reached Wannsee where a single-engine plane was waiting on a deserted street. The propeller came to life and roared for a few minutes until the pilot maneuvered the plane to a broader street and accelerated. The plane lifted up uneasily and disappeared into the smoke and clouds.

I headed for the Munich train station in the morning, boarded my train, and caught a little sleep on the way. Berlin had not rebuilt as quickly as Munich. That was clear as I walked from the train station, map in hand, to the east, just past the Brandenburg Gate where Russian women were directing traffic while American MPs and tourists looked on. I came to place but could not find what I was looking for. Nonetheless, there was an odious feel to the place.

A passerby looked at me suspiciously. "It was demolished a few years ago. I am glad they did and so should you."

"You may be sure I am glad it's no longer here," I replied as I consulted the map. I proceeded south. With each step I felt the presence and when I reached the broad streets of Wannsee I whispered despairingly, "He's alive. I know it. God help us. He's alive."

Back in Munich I telephoned Stefan Walter and frantically asked him to come by as I was exhausted but had something urgent to tell him. He said he was busy but would come by after work. True to his word he arrived about six and we sat in the parlor.

"Stefan, you have worked with me for quite some time and you have found my gift useful. I have offered you senses, thoughts, perceptions, then your group probes deeper."

"Very useful. You know that. With your help we have found corroborative witnesses and brought men to justice, though I must say the sentences are too often lenient."

"Then I hope what I am about to say will not be dismissed as hysterical nonsense from a reader of tea leaves."

"No, of course not. But where is this going, Bertha? Your agitation surprises me. And it worries me as well."

"Stefan, what happened in the Führerbunker at the end of the war? What became of Hitler?"

"He killed himself. The Soviets burned the body and scatted the ashes along the Elbe. Oh, Bertha, please do not tell me!"

"I went into the sea a few days ago and I saw Hitler escaping from the bunker and flying out of Berlin in a small plane."

"Oh, Bertha. To where? Where could he flee? Where could he hide?"

"I have not determined that yet. I tell you I traveled to Berlin yesterday and went to the site of the Führerbunker."

"It was razed years go! The Soviets did it to prevent it becoming a shrine for the remaining fanatics."

"I know, I know. I saw the vacant space and curious onlookers. I felt his presence leaving the bunker under heavy fire and making his way to Wannsee where a plane was waiting for him. I retraced his path and felt him with every step I took. I had to look around to make sure he was not behind me. I knew him, Stefan! I met with him several times and misled him every time! I developed a sense for his evil spirit. It's still out there, waiting!"

Stefan sat back in his chair and eyed me uneasily. I had never told him anything about meeting Hitler and revealing it now was not easy to accept. Nor was it helpful in convincing him of my conviction.

"There are so many stories and rumors and whispers. They are all either Soviet propaganda that tries to convince gullible people that the West is evil and the USSR won the war on its own. Or they are the hopes of old believers and young nihilists. That is what you sensed. The aspirations of Germans who have to hide their thoughts because they are so outlandish and foolish. Their beliefs live on, though in muted forms, but their Führer is dead."

"I know this, Stefan! Of course I do! But I feel he is out there still, waiting for his day to return."

"His day is over and it will never return, Bertha. Now please, get some rest. And of course if you have any further information you know how to get in touch with me."

I closed myself in, unplugged the radio, and fasted two days again. I looked out onto the streets half expecting a strange visitor or an unfamiliar car parked outside. Munich was quiet. It was 3am.

I was ready to go deep into the sea, far deeper than before. During those sessions I felt there were recesses to explore but I always held back. I saw what I or a client wanted to learn, then came back to this world and put what I saw into words, sometimes with great relief.

That night I let myself drift further and further out until I heard an immense swirling eddy close by. Whooshing sounds mixed with thunder. I thought of the last time I met him in the chateau outside Berlin when we stared into each other. His eyes, his eyes, his eyes....

A Spanish-style villa surrounded by thick tropical foliage and triple-canopy trees...an indigenous guard detail is supervised by a large-framed German. The interior is that of a prosperous planation of years past. The rattan furnishings are untidily placed and some have been hurled about. A dark corridor with pictures of Prussian generals and baroque monuments on the walls. A dimly-lit study where a ceiling fan creaks and hums as it makes lazy turns.

He sits there, sick, alone, and desolate, as he writes with shaky hand before stopping and looking at a Luger next to the notepad.

"Betrayed…betrayed by all around me. They failed me…they failed their nation. The Jew witch was right about them. And about me."

He was on the brink, weighing life and death, his self-pity and narcissism in earnest combat.

"My eyes," I said intently. "Remember my eyes, their attraction, their power. Think of them now. Think of them burrowing into your soul the way they did in Munich and Charlottenburg. We were connected, one might say intimate. And we are connected now. You know the path. The only path to dignity and eternal glory. Take it! Take it now!"

He held the pistol in his palsied hand and admired its gleaming metal and walnut handle.

"Take it! Take it now!"

He pulled the bolt back to chamber a round, closed his eyes, and placed the muzzle to his temple.

"Your soldiers await you. Germany awaits you."

He threw the papers across the room and wept like a spoiled child.

"I have an unalterable will, you Jew witch!"

"Take it! Take it now! It is your unalterable will that tells you this! Bertha's word!"

He became calm and nodded slowly.

The guard detail heard a shot and the German ran inside.

I woke up to the sound of traffic. It was late morning on a beautiful day. Munich never looked so wondrous.

BERTHA'S FINAL WORD

"That's my story, Dani. My life before, during, and after the Third Reich. I mentioned some of these episodes to people, including your father and his friends at the seafront cafe."

"The Knesset, Bertha. My father and his friends call themselves the Knesset."

"And a fine deliberative body it is. So many wonderful people. You, Dani, are also a wonderful person. That is why I chose you to hear the whole story, not just a few words in-between bites of baklava."

"I am honored, Bertha, and deeply touched. I shall cherish the gift of your life story forever."

"I knew you would," she said with a sweet smile. "I just knew it."

"What of Nadia? Have you told her?"

"Yes and no. She knows more than the Knesset, less than you. I held back, Dani. There are those around us who would hear my story and become enraged. They would think I was a willing assistant to the Nazi regime and an equally willing mistress to an SS monster. I could never convince anyone that Reinhard Beck had a decent heart. People do not see complications and nuances. That are given to anger and self-righteousness."

"Sad but true, Bertha. You helped shorten the war."

"Perhaps, perhaps. I like to think I did. I spent hours a day back then thinking matters through and formulating how to present a path to ruin to them. No one looks to the past anymore. Everything is in the present. That's our world – and soon I will be leaving it."

My instinctual response was called off instantly by the honesty we felt when we looked at each other.

"You would know, of course."

"That is true, that is true." She smiled quirkily "I've had a good life. I have seen great events and met – " Thoughts and images halted her. She paused to find words.

"Have you ever looked at a person, someone you did not know, and thought if only for a moment that you had some connection to that person? I was in the same room with him, Adolf Hitler – in Munich and outside Berlin. I read him, I sensed who he was, I felt his presence. He was mad, he was evil. That was clear and we all know it. He had immense personal power, magnetism, what the sociologists call charisma. There was a malevolent and timeless force dwelling in his soul. It was there from birth, from conception, and brought down from a dark period centuries ago to plague our time. That force saw that he lived through the First World War, became master of much of Europe, and survived all those attempts on his life. Think of it, Dani. Professional military men could not kill him. It was that malevolent force dwelling inside him, protecting him."

"Did he recognize that you saw this malevolent force inside him? Did he recognize an opposite timeless force inside you?"

"Oh yes. We understood each other and he saw my gift. Not simply from what he had been told by others or from what I said to him. He saw that I had something innate too. It was not evil or thirst for power and death. It was the ability to transcend the world and see beyond today. For all his personal power he could not do that and powerful though he was, he was nagged by doubts and insecurities. So this young Jewish woman had power over him and that is how she survived."

She heaved a slow, weak sigh. "I am ready to go, Dani. My story is in good hands."

"I will treasure it as long as I live."

"Ahh. A long time then."

"Bertha's word?"

"Bertha's word."

She drifted off to sleep. With tears in my eyes, I leaned down and kissed her forehead.

Two days later my phone rang. I knew it was Nadia and also the reason for her call.

"My mother died this morning in her sleep, "she said calmly. She wants a small funeral with only a handful of family members. Sorry."

"Don't be. It was her wish and I respect it. If I can be of any help, please let me know."

"Perhaps next week."

She hung up.

Though I knew Bertha's time had been at hand, the word of her passing grieved me. I sat back and wept and stopped only upon sensing her presence and her fondness for me.

I listened to some of the tapes recorded in the hospital over the next few days. I felt blessed to have known her. Her story was all there. No one else knew what I knew, at least not all of it, not even her daughter. I naturally wondered if Nadia knew what I knew about her father. I felt certain she did not and considered if I should reveal that information some day.

Nadia called not long after the interment to tell me of an envelope her mother had left for me. Moved and intrigued, I drove out to her house in Kfar Neter, not far from her mother's home. She invited me to her backyard where pine trees shaded us from the summer sun. I asked how her mother's funeral went and she said it was beautiful but offered no details.

Not wanting my visit to be long, she handed me a manila envelope. Its contents, judging by weight and touch, were not much more than a page or two.

"She wanted you to open it in my presence."

Inside was a photograph – black and white, yellowed with age, with a few creases here and there but not on the face. It was an SS officer with four pips on his collar. His face had a warmth you do not associate with his organization. It could easily be thought of that of a gentle farmer or musician. I knew who it was even before I turned it over and saw the name.

"Reinhard Beck"

Bertha's final message was clear. Fulfilling it just then presented matters of tact which I am not practiced in. I looked at her to find a way to begin.

"Never mind. I know who that man is. That is the man fate and circumstances chose to be my father."

"Your mother told you then."

"No, she did not. However, Daniel, she did pass on a gift to me."

"Ahh... the gift."

"I have one simple request before you leave, Daniel."

"Of course. Anything."

"I would like to keep the photograph."

"It's yours then."

"Thank you. This I believe to be our last meeting and I would like to leave you with a message my mother asked me to give you the night before she died."

Another jarring moment, though a touching one that brought me near tears.

"She said your marriage was troubled in recent months and she wanted to see you through it, but could not. She counsels that you and your wife see things through. You can and will. She loves you and you love her. Listen to her. Let her tell you what bothers her. She will do the same. You belong to each other. You will get through this and stay together for the rest of your lives."

I had never discussed my marriage with Bertha, not in so many words anyway. I was not surprised she sensed it though. Not in the least.

"Mother is certain that you and your wife will see it through."

I nodded. There was nothing else to do but nod and smile bravely and stand to leave.

"Bertha's word," Nadia added unexpectedly.

Bertha's presence swept through me, filling me with joy and hope and confidence. I bade Nadia a farewell and returned to my car for the long drive. I arrived home sooner than I thought. My wife was waiting for me.

"Is everything alright, Dani?"

I pressed her to my heart. We hadn't embraced as fondly in months.

Printed in the United States
by Baker & Taylor Publisher Services

Printed in the United States
by Baker & Taylor Publisher Services